BEGINNING IN ARCHAEOLOGY

Three-dimensional recording with triangle and plumb-bob.

Beginning in Archaeology

by

KATHLEEN M. KENYON

Revised edition,
with sections on American archaeology
by Saul S. and Gladys D. Weinberg

FREDERICK A. PRAEGER, *Publishers*

New York • Washington

BOOKS THAT MATTER

Published in the United States of America in 1957 by
Frederick A. Praeger, Publishers
111 Fourth Avenue, New York, N.Y. 10003

Third printing, 1966

The original edition of this book was published in 1952 by
Frederick A. Praeger, Inc., New York. A second, enlarged
edition was published in 1953. The present edition contains
further revisions

Library of Congress Catalog Card Number: 53–11325

Printed in the United States of America

CONTENTS

ILLUSTRATIONS

Acknowledgements are due to *The Society of Antiquaries* for the use of plates nos 2, 3, 4, 5, 7, 8, and 9 and to *The Palestine Exploration Fund* for Fig. 6.

FOREWORD

MY PRINCIPAL qualification to write a book entitled *Beginning in Archaeology* is that in the course of my tenure of office as Secretary of the Institute of Archaeology of the University of London I have been asked for advice by many would-be beginners, and that both in that capacity and as a Director of Excavations I have assisted in the initial training of many beginners. I therefore feel, in the first place, that I do know the kind of questions which would-be-beginners ask, and the kind of questions which they have to be asked. In the earlier chapters I have tried to provide some of the answers. In the second place, I do know the sort of knowledge I would like a beginner on a dig to have acquired beforehand, so as to lighten my work in training him, and the later chapters try to provide this information.

In writing a book of which the title covers such a wide field, one has to touch on subjects of which one has only a general knowledge. In the matter of excavations, I can write with first-hand knowledge of most but not all of the main types of digs, but it must be emphasized that no one school of excavation has a monopoly of correct methods, and I can only describe the methods of the school in which I have been trained. In the matter of fields of archaeology I can write with first-hand knowledge only of a limited number, and my remarks on the others can only be of a general nature. But such is the complexity of modern archaeology that anyone else would have to confess to the same limitations, and that is my excuse for attempting it.

In writing such a book I have of course drawn on the experience and knowledge of my own teachers and many colleagues. But I must acknowledge my indebtedness to two in particular, my two chiefs as Directors of the Institute of Archaeology, Sir R. E. Mortimer Wheeler, to whom I owe all my training in field archaeology and constant inspiration towards improved methods, and the late Professor V. Gordon Childe, whose brilliant analyses and syntheses of archaeological subjects are such a stimulus to a broad view.

For the enlarged edition I am also grateful for the contribution from my American colleagues, Saul and Gladys Weinberg.

K.M.K.

I

The Meaning of Archaeology

To some people, the word archaeology suggests something as dry as dust, a pursuit followed by elderly, long-bearded professors; to others the word is full of romance, suggesting buried treasure, a life in the wide-open spaces, and buried cities revealed by the spade. Neither idea is very close to the truth. Archaeology is a scientific study, and as such, involves skilled and laborious work. Sometimes startling discoveries are made, such as that of Tutankhamen's tomb, but, almost without exception, they are the reward of many years' work without spectacular results, as was indeed the case in the discovery of this tomb. Moreover, most archaeologists are not working with the expectation of finding a king's tomb or similar riches. They are aiming at throwing light on some portion of man's past by the careful piecing together of evidence, much of it apparently insignificant in itself. But in this there is nevertheless romance, though not that of the treasure hunt. It is, at any rate, safe to say that those who embark on archaeology are generally fascinated and seldom bored.

Readers of this book will probably be only those who expect to find archaeology interesting, so that it is not necessary to spend any time in attempting to convert the dry-as-dust school. The aim of this book is to explain what archaeology is, how one can set about becoming an archaeologist, and to give an introduction to archaeological methods as an aid to, but not a substitute for, practical experience.

To begin with, archaeology is not an end in itself, not just an abstract study. It is the method of finding out about the past of the human race in its material aspects, and the study of the products of this past. These aspects may be the way people lived, the way they worshipped, the way they built, their art, their trade, their travels. All these aspects are of course studied by historians. But historians are concerned primarily with written records, and the earliest systems of writing were only invented some five thousand years ago, whereas man was evolved from his ape-like ancestors about half-a-million years ago. In the study of man during this immensely long period, archaeology is necessary, for archaeology deals with all the material remains of man, the objects he used and made, his dwelling places and defensive structures, his tools and weapons, the remains of his food, his own bones and burial places, and, from these, deduces how he lived. Thus archaeology provides the information for the prehistory of man, his history before the beginnings of written records.

But its use does not stop when written records begin. In the first place, many written records are only found in the course of archaeological investigations. Even when they are found, they are usually biased, and do not tell us all that we want to know about our predecessors and ancestors. For one thing, writing developed very much earlier in some areas than others. In Mesopotamia and Egypt writing was widely developed in the third millenium B.C., whereas in Britain we have little evidence of its use before the Roman invasion in the first century A.D. Then, the majority of early records are concerned with the great affairs of state, the accounts of the great temples and the expeditions of the kings; far fewer tell us how ordinary people lived. Roman writers describe some events in Britain during the three hundred and fifty years of Roman rule there, but Britain was a small and far-distant part of the Empire, in which most Roman historians had not a great deal of interest, so that we should have a very bare and one-sided picture of this period in Britain without the aid of archaeology.

Thus archaeology covers a very wide sphere both in time, space and subject matter, and though the same basic principles of study apply throughout, they have to be adapted to deal with different circumstances, a subject which will be discussed in later chapters. Here we are concerned with the broad meaning of archaeology, and with its scope in general terms. As will be seen, different archaeologists, whether professional or amateur, can, and indeed must, specialise in different aspects, but they are all contributing to knowledge within the general framework.

To learn something about a group of people, one of the first things we should want to know is the environment in which they lived, that is to say, whether they lived as hunters in clearings in a forest, as herdsmen on open downs, as importers of food from foreign countries, and so on. Obviously, if you were investigating the villa of a rich man living in Italy, you would know much of this from literary sources; if you were concerned with a similar villa in Roman Britain, you would know much less. At the other extreme, if you were investigating an unknown group of primitive tribesmen, you would know nothing at all beforehand.

The environment of a group of primitive people can be established by finding out what the climate was, what sort of vegetation they had to deal with, what wild or domesticated animals there were, and whether they had any cultivated crops. The identification of the animals is obviously comparatively simple, for the bones associated with the occupied sites can be identified, and it can usually be said whether they belong to wild or domesticated animals. This may give one clue as to the natural vegetation conditions, as different types of animals thrive in different conditions; pigs, for instance, like forests, whereas sheep like open down-land. In suitable conditions, evidence of the actual vegetation can be recovered. Such conditions are provided by deposits of peat, in which the pollen grains of the contemporary vegetation are preserved. Analysis of this will show what were the trees and plants growing in the neighbourhood, and from this the type of climate can be established, and even, from the type of weeds growing, whether land had been cleared for cultivation in the neighbourhood. In dealing with less primitive groups, evidence from the animal bones will show whether reliance was placed entirely on stock-breeding, or whether it was supplemented by hunting. Specimens of the types of grain grown shows to what extent agriculture was practised, while the finding of agricultural implements and of evidence for storage shows what methods were used.

At very few stages in human history did groups live as isolated units. They traded inventions and products, fought each other, imposed their rule on weaker groups and so on, while a prosperous and fertile group may send out offshoots to acquire new land and spread the ways of the parent group far afield. Therefore, the next task of the archaeologist is to establish the cultural affinities of the group with which he is dealing. Man is so much a slave of habit, that fashions in making implements, ornaments and objects of daily use can very often be used as evidence of connections between groups in culture, race, or at least trade. When the objects in use among a group have been identified, the next task is to see where else similar ones are found, and thus with what other groups the one in question has been in contact. In this, household pottery is one of the most useful categories, for once it was invented, it became extremely common with most groups, was often broken and its fragments left lying about, while different shapes and wares can be shown to be associated with different groups of people. Thus if a new type of pottery suddenly appears in one area, it is fairly certain that it was brought by newcomers, as traders or invaders, and when the other places where such pottery occurs can be traced, the place of origin of the newcomers can usually be discovered. On the other hand, the appearance of an isolated object, such as a bead or a brooch, can, as a rule, be ascribed to trade, and a study of the distribution of such objects can establish the trade-routes in use.

The archaeologist must also, of course, find out how the people he is dealing with lived, in the broadest sense. To give a complete picture, he must try to find the evidence for their social organisation. In a primitive community, the presence of one very large hut in the centre of a village, surrounded by other smaller ones, suggests some form of chieftainship or aristocratic rule. Similarly, an area in which there appear to be only a few large and complex Roman villas, with quarters for serfs or dependents, suggests an agricultural system based on great landed estates, whereas one in which there are only comparatively simple villas of farmhouse type, suggests peasant or yeoman smallholdings. This is the sort of information which, in the case of Roman Britain, can be obtained only from archaeology and not from the written sources.

Religion is another subject on which archaeology provides a very great deal of information. For primitive religion, of the sort that is represented by the paintings of the Stone Age found in the French and Spanish caves, by monuments such as Stonehenge, or by the burial rites which can be deduced from the great sepulchral mounds found on the Cotswolds, archaeology is the only source of information. But even for religion of countries for which we have much literary evidence, such as Mesopotamia, Egypt and Palestine, archaeology does much to make the literary allusions and descriptions clear. The Bible is full of allusions to the religion of the Canaanites, against which the Israelites had to maintain such a constant struggle, but many of the allusions are obscure, since explanations were unnecessary to people who were familiar with the subject. Archaeological discoveries of Canaanite High Places, Horns of the Altar, pillars of Ashtoreth and so on, have made many of these allusions clear, while the study of Semitic religion, in the texts discovered in excavations and in the material remains of the cults, has shown the background against which the religion of the Israelites developed. Again, we know a great deal about the religion of Greece and Rome from literary sources, but of the more obscure aspects of it we should know nothing without archaeology. The discovery of a number of temples of a type peculiar to Britain and northern Gaul shows how classical religious practices were adapted by the Celts, and the identification in Britain of temples dedicated to the Asia Minor dieties of Atis and Cybele and the Eastern god Mithras, shows how these exotic cults obtained a foothold there.

In throwing light on the religion of early peoples, archaeology is even, from the evidence of material remains, showing us something of the way their minds worked. The same can be said for the evidence it produces about their art, much of which is closely connected with religion. This art may range from the crude female figurines carved by primitive man, to the great palace reliefs of the Assyrian kings or the sculptures of classical Greece. A study of them reveals both the technical skill of the artists and the ideas which were in their minds when executing them. Some of the results are great in themselves and by all standards. Others are the efforts of crude local craftsmen to express themselves, but even these are most valuable evidence as to the way men were living and thinking at the time.

The foregoing paragraphs are an attempt to show what the archaeologist is after when he sets out to examine the remains of some past people. He is not looking for a vanished town in an unexplored wilderness, or digging one out of the soil which has covered it, just for the sake of finding it. Having found it, he goes on to discover everything he can about the people who lived in it. Again he may be studying one particular class of objects, for instance a type of coin, but this is not as an end in itself, it is to discover by its distribution the region controlled by a particular dynasty, or to show the economic basis reflected by the answers to the problem he is studying. It is very exciting to make a discovery like that of Tutankhamen's tomb, and to provide beautiful objects to be admired in museums. But having discovered it, and safely extracted all the delicate objects, the archaeologists' task, or that of his collaborators, is only just beginning. The religious practices which dictated the placing of the objects in the tomb, the craftsmanship and technique in the manufacture of the objects, the representations of everyday life and ceremonial, the evidence of trade in materials or manufactured works of art; all these and many other problems have got to be studied, in order that the find can make its full contribution to knowledge.

It will thus be clear that archaeology is a many-sided affair, and its methods are necessarily equally varied. Basically, it is a matter of discovering ancient materials and studying them in order to throw as much light on their makers and users as possible. Many ancient objects come to light quite fortuitously. Greek sculptures and vases are discovered in Italy, brought there by ancient or Renaissance art lovers. A stone axe is found in a heap of gravel, a bronze dagger in a river bed. All these objects are interesting and may be artistically or technologically important. But they are far more so if they are found *in situ*, in the temple of which the statue was the cult object, or in the grave in which was buried the owner of the dagger. Therefore, the primary method of archaeology is exploration and excavation. As will be seen in a later chapter, it is not always necessary to dig up ancient remains in order to obtain information of value. Much can be deduced from a study of the distribution of remains visible on the surface.

Nevertheless, full information can rarely be obtained without clearing and excavation. It is the excavator, for the most part, who provides the material on which his colleagues work, and therefore to most people the description archaeologist suggests someone who digs. He provides the framework, by producing the evidence that, on a particular site, a group of people lived in a particular way and used particular objects. From this evidence, the conclusions which have been suggested in the preceding paragraphs can be drawn. The objects he has found can be studied and inferences deduced from them. Much of this will be done by the excavator himself, and some of it must be. Other subjects, such as works of art, coins, problems of technology, may be referred to experts in these particular fields. When the results are all assembled and properly published, other archaeologists, who possibly may not themselves ever excavate, can combine the results into a bigger picture of some aspect of the subject, and so put together another chapter of prehistory, or supplement some aspect of history. The term archaeologist therefore covers a large number of specialists and students in different subjects and branches, though for the most part they are dependent on the archaeologist who digs to provide them with material for their studies.

II

The Framework of Archaeology

THIS IS NOT the place to attempt to give an outline of the past cultures and civilisations with the study of which archaeology is concerned. But in order to grasp what archaeology is, and therefore what one is proposing to do when 'beginning in archaeology', one must have an idea of what the subject covers. Without this, a beginner cannot make up his or her mind as to the field which seems to offer the greatest interest, nor understand the description of methods in the following chapters.

The first thing which must be grasped is the meaning of the stages in man's development which form the framework of modern archaeology. This framework is provided by the great divisions of the Palaeolithic, Mesolithic, Neolithic, Bronze and Iron Ages. These names are based on the principal materials men used for their tools and weapons, stone being used during the first three with distinguishing techniques, and in the last two, metals. Yet though these facts are important, there are many other factors which are equally or more important.

The first stage, the Palaeolithic, lasted for tens, even hundreds of thousands of years. The older archaeologists distinguished it as the period in which men made their implements of chipped stone. But as we know it now, we see that it is the stage when man is only slowly differentiating himself from the rest of the animal world, and is still, like it, depending on the food which nature has provided, the other animals and the wild vegetables. He is, in fact, a hunter and food-gatherer, living, like an animal, in small family groups. But he is already differentiated from the animals by the fact that he has learnt to make tools which help him to hunt and to gather his food, and he does not have to depend only on bodily strength or

16

sharpness of tooth or nail. He can therefore develop physically in a way the animals cannot, for his bodily efficiency can be all-round and not concentrated on one thing only. His mental powers develop at the same time, for inventiveness in tools, clothes and so on reap their own reward, and give their owners the best chance of survival.

During this stage in the evolution of man, Europe and Asia, the homes of early man, were in the grip of the Ice Age. The ice cap of the Arctic extended very much further south than it does today, covering very nearly the whole of Britain and central Europe, with other ice-caps extending out from the Alps and other high mountains. Over periods of tens of thousands of years, the ice-caps advanced and retreated in periods of maximum cold and milder intervening periods. With the advances and retreats, men and animals changed their habitats as the climate and vegetation altered. Much of the first stages of the evolution of man is still uncertain. There seem, however, to have been several species of man, distinguished by differences in their skeletal formations and by their techniques in making their stone tools and weapons. Some species seem to have been better adapted to cold conditions than others. But by the last stage the real ancestor of modern man, *homo sapiens*, dominates the field and the other species die out.

As might be expected in such climatic conditions, men lived in the most sheltered positions they could find, and most of the best remains we find are in caves. It is, in fact, with few exceptions only in caves that we can hope to find the remains of Palaeolithic man *in situ*. Over the very long period of time represented by the Palaeolithic Age, great changes in the surface of the earth took place. The relative levels of land and sea changed several times, river beds cut down through pre-existing deposits, or deposited fresh soil on older surfaces, glaciers planed off the surface of the land in one area, and formed great moraines in others, so that the whole face of the land was changed out of recognition. These changes swept away most of the traces of man's occupation. But, however drastic the movements, it was almost impossible to destroy the products of man's labour, the stone implements after which the period has been named. Therefore, in the glacial moraines and the gravels of ancient river terraces we find these implements, sometimes together with contemporary human or animal bones. Such deposits, with caves, are our principal source of the remains of this period. Obviously, however, we cannot in these circumstances expect to discover much about how the men of the period lived.

At last, some twelve thousand years ago or less, the ice-cap finally receded to something like its present position. The change did not, as might be expected, immediately benefit the human race. Great forests started to cover the now temperate zone, and the animals which Palaeolithic men had hunted followed the edges of the retreating ice cap, for they could not, as man could, adapt themselves to the new temperate forest life. The Mesolithic Age, which followed the end of the glacial periods, is in some ways rather a poor, struggling stage in man's development, in which he is adapting himself to a new environment. He is still a hunter and food gatherer, but has a less well-stocked preserve in which to hunt. Some groups seem to have lived mainly on fish, some on shell-fish, and others on the birds and small animals found in forests.

But about ten thousand years ago man began to make the first great discoveries from which modern civilisation has developed. This stage is called the Neolithic, because when the stages of man's development were first being worked out in Europe, the fact which suggested the start of a new epoch to archaeologists was the appearance of a new way of making stone implements, by grinding and polishing them, instead of just chipping them. But though in some areas this new technique does appear at this period, it is not nearly as important as a great many other new developments.

It is at this stage that the Near East assumes the important position in human progress which it occupies for the next eight thousand years, for it is fairly certain that these new developments took place somewhere in this area. The basic change was the transformation of man from a food gatherer to a food producer, for this had consequences of the most far-reaching kind. As climatic conditions in Europe improved, the rain belts which had covered North Africa and southern Asia moved northwards, and present-day dry and desert conditions began to be established in those areas. This led to a contraction of the area in which man could live, and forced the wandering hunters and food-gatherers to draw closer together, particularly in the river valleys and oases. Such a concentration of population naturally limited the food available to the hunters. But at the same time, animals tended to concentrate in the same areas, and be brought into closer proximity to man, and thus the idea of domesticating them must have arisen.

In the same way, since groups were now more sedentary, the idea must have arisen of increasing the vegetable foods by planting and cultivating them near the settlement of the group, and thus agriculture arose. That this was somewhere in the Near East is shown by the fact that it is here that the types of grain first cultivated grow wild, and it is in the same area that are found the ancestors of domesticated cattle and sheep.

The change was no doubt a very gradual one. Groups would continue to hunt as well as to farm and raise cattle. We do not know where the new discoveries were made, whether they were made in several places independently, nor whether agriculture and stock breeding were developed approximately contemporaneously. For long, no doubt, groups living in the old and the new ways existed side by side.

But gradually the new developments spread and asserted themselves, until we find a network of Neolithic villages spread over a large area of the Near East. The contrast between such groups and those of the earlier stage is that they could live a settled life and produce their own food. The contrast between them and those of the subsequent stages is that they were comparatively self-sufficient. Their needs were simple and they could be satisfied within the resources of the group. Gradually a number of inventions were made, such as the manufacture of pottery and spinning and weaving, and all these industries could be carried out within the confines of the village.

Our knowledge of this whole process is still very incomplete. Recent excavations have shown that at Jericho Mesolithic hunters began to settle down soon after 8000 B.C., and by 7000 B.C. their descendants were living in a walled town about ten acres in size.

Other groups may have been equally progressive, but in the majority of cases the transition was slower, and as late as the fifth millennium most of the settlements in Western Asia were small, self-sufficient villages.

As we have seen, these new developments took place in the Near East. But from there they spread gradually in all directions, in due course reaching places as far afield as Britain. Some of this spread may have been due to ideas passing from group to group, as good ideas do. Some was certainly due to the migration of groups. Primitive agriculture is destructive of the fertility of the soil, and after a period a village would have to move to fresh ground. Also, only a limited population could, in primitive conditions, be supported on the land round any one village, and as the population increased, groups would have to hive off and form fresh communities, and thus the new ideas were gradually brought to fresh areas. As this new sedentary and agricultural way of life reached temperate Europe, forests would gradually be cleared to make fields, and the country slowly be opened up.

While the Neolithic phase was spreading across Europe, new developments were taking place in the Near East. There were two factors in these new developments, the growth of towns and the discovery of the use of metal. As with the developments which brought about the Neolithic revolution, physical and geographical factors were of great importance in the growth of towns. That took place at this stage in the great river valleys of the Near East, especially that of the Nile in Egypt and those of the Tigris and Euphrates in Mesopotamia. The same is probably true of the Indus valley further east, but less is known of the beginnings of the process there. In these valleys, the rivers gave fertility to the soil. Therefore, far bigger communities could be supported than elsewhere, and thus towns were made possible. But at the same time the behaviour of the rivers, especially their liability to flood, made it desirable to have some communal organisation to control them, to dig canals and flood-banks and to prevent silting. Organisation of irrigation, again, increased the fertile areas. Such organisation required leaders, and thus in these embryo towns elected or hereditary rulers began to appear. Since primitive man had early ascribed the acts of nature to some form of divine power, these early rulers were usually associated with religious functions, as interceding with the divinities so that the course of nature should be favourable; and thus priest-kings arose.

An important result of this development of towns was the creation of surplus supplies of food through increased efficiency in the cultivation of the land. The importance of this is connected with the other great development, the discovery of the use of copper, and of the improved quality of metal tools and weapons as compared with those of stone, particularly when the copper is mixed with tin to form bronze. Now stone is available almost everywhere, whereas copper and tin only occur in limited areas. Therefore copper and tin had to be obtained by trade. Also the smelting and casting of the metal were skilled jobs, not to be carried out by most members of the population for themselves, and so professional traders and specialist smiths were needed. These specialists were only the first of many: potters, wheelwrights, artists and a large number of others. Such craftsmen as these had not time to grow their own food, so the remainder of the population needed surpluses of food to exchange with the specialists for their products. Surpluses were most readily available in the growing towns of the great river valleys, where at the same time mineral wealth was not as a rule locally obtainable and thus the development of the commercial and agricultural resources of these towns and, incidentally, of their prestige became a condition of their existence.

In this way the comparatively static self-sufficiency of the Neolithic villages began to break down. The change was a very gradual one, with many degrees of transition, but once started, the process was steady. As with the Neolithic revolution, the new developments spread outwards from their centre in the Near East, and followed the same general routes across Europe.

The development of towns in the river valleys was followed by the gradual establishment of city states and then empires, as the growing towns competed with each other and conquered each other, until by about 3000 B.C., we find the first great empires of Egypt and Mesopotamia being formed. While Europe was still gradually receiving the Neolithic and Bronze Age stages of culture, in the Near East great civilisations arose. The priests and rulers, in whose hands most of the surpluses accumulated, had to invent systems of recording the wealth of the temple or state, and writing and arithmetic were developed. Laws for the management of the state had to be made, and important events recorded, and thus legal systems and historical records arose. Records needed a chronological framework. The seasons in particular had to be calculated in advance, and in Egypt the annual rise of the river, so calendars were established, of which more will be said shortly.

Round about 1200 B.C., the introduction of iron in place of bronze made tools and weapons much cheaper, for iron is more plentiful than copper. The significance of the beginning of the Iron Age is not, however, as great as that of the Bronze Age, for it did not imply a social revolution. The difference was in degree rather than kind. As with the earlier discoveries, it spread outwards from the east over Europe.

The interplay between the great civilisations of the river valleys of the Near East is the background of the history of the area for some three thousand years. In due course, other rivals arose, but it was not until the Greek and then the Roman civilisations developed, each of them owing much to their great predecessors, that the balance of power and leadership in the progress of civilisation began to move west. And it was not until the Romans conquered most of north-western Europe that all the developments of Eastern and Mediterranean civilisation reached that area, which had gradually absorbed in turn the new inventions and discoveries of the Neolithic, Bronze and Iron Ages. Archaeology does not, of course, stop at this point, but succeeding developments are comparatively familiar from the history book, and need not be outlined here.

This description of the development of the different phases in human progress is necessarily summary in the extreme, but the aim has been to give some idea of the framework into which the archaeology and prehistory of each country fits, and of the broad characteristics of the principal phases. There is one other part of the framework which requires consideration, and that is dating. Nowadays, we can say with some confidence that the beginning of the First Dynasty of Egypt can be dated round about 3000 B.C. (actually experts differ between 3200 and 2900 B.C.), or that the Early Bronze Age in Britain begins about 1800 B.C. What is the basis for these statements?

Basically, all such datings go back to the dating systems established by the great empires of the Near East. As the city states and then kingdoms increased in complexity of organisation the need for some chronological basis for records became apparent, and also some method for calculating the seasons. This was particularly necessary in Egypt, where the whole agricultural routine was based on the annual risings of the Nile, and the rulers and their subjects had to know when this was to be expected. Therefore a system based on observation of the stars was worked out, and on this system was based the records of the reigns of the kings. Modern scholars have been able to correlate these records with our present calendar within a small margin of error. As king-lists and other historical documents are from time to time discovered, the greater part of the countries of the Near East have on this basis been provided with a chronological framework which is reasonably accurate from about 3000 B.C.

But these methods can obviously not be applied to those countires for which there are no written records, that is to say, to most of Europe for the subsequent three thousand years. Britain, for instance, does not come within the orbit of historical records with a fixed chronology until the Roman conquest in A.D. 43, apart from a brief reference in connection with the Caesarian raids of 55-54 B.C. Therefore, absolute dates for stages of development in Europe in this period can only be fixed by contacts with the civilisations of the Near East or Mediterranean for which a chronological framework has been established. One method by which this can be done is by actual references in historical records. An example of this is the evidence in Caesar's account of his invasion of Britain that the Belgic tribes had only established themselves in the south-eastern part of the country within living memory, and we can thus fix their occupation of this area to about 75 B.C. Another example is the historical evidence for the foundation of Greek colonies in

Southern Italy in the eighth century B.C. This gives key points for
the dating of the Italian Iron Age, which greatly influenced the first
stage of the Iron Age north of the Alps, and the whole of the
chronology of the European Iron Age is largely dependent on this
dating.

Such historical evidence is, however, rare, increasingly so for the
earlier periods. Other evidence of contacts fortunately comes from
trade, for even in quite remote periods, objects which can be dated
to a definite period in a Mediterranean or eastern country found their
way north and west, where they have been discovered in association
with the objects of the native civilisation. These can therefore be
shown to be either contemporary with the period of use of those
objects in their home country, or, more probably, slightly later,
since there may have been a certain amount of time lag in the arrival
of the imports in the place where they are found. Sometimes, even,
exports from the northern and western countries are also found in
the countries with historical records, and thus a cross check is provided, and the dating can become more accurate. An example of the
appearance of Mediterranean objects in northern surroundings is the
finding of a type of segmented faience bead, known in the period of
the Eighteenth Dynasty in Egypt, in burials in Britain of the Middle
Bronze Age, which on these and similar grounds are dated to about
1400 B.C. Other deductions too can be made from the evidence
for the migration of groups which can be connected with similar
groups in the Near East. In these ways, by a careful correlation of
many items of evidence, a chronological framework for a large part
of the later European prehistoric period has been built up, not of
course so detailed or accurate as that of the Near East, but nevertheless reasonably fixed.

For the earlier periods, including the whole of the Palaeolithic
and Mesolithic periods, such methods clearly cannot be employed,
since at this time there was no contemporary historical record with
which stages of development could be correlated. For these periods,
largely geological evidence has to be employed. Geologists and
geochronologists have been able to provide a broad chronological
framework for the advance and retreat of the ice-cap during the

glacial period. The deposits in which human remains have been found can usually be related to one or other of these glacial phases, and the type of implement, or of human skeleton, can thus be shown to belong to that phase. Evidence is also given by the kind of animals with which the human material was associated, showing whether it belongs to a warm or cold phase. The fluctuations in climate which followed the end of the glacial age are reflected by the type of vegetation, trees and plants which like cold, damp or warm climates, and the pollen shed by them can be found in soils which accumulated during that climatic phase. The association of objects of human origin with evidence of particular kinds of vegetation thus dates that human material to a particular climatic phase, which can be roughly dated by geochronologists. In this way, evidence is provided for the dating of Mesolithic and early Neolithic man, down to the time when contacts begin to be established with the datable civilisations of the Near East.

The most recent addition to methods of establishing the date of remote periods is the use of measurements of Carbon 14 (radioactive carbon) in objects contained in deposits belonging to the period in question. All living organisms contain Carbon 14, and the rate at which their radioactivity is lost has been established. The surviving activity of ancient organic matter can be measured, and thus its age calculated. At present datings can only be given within margins of a hundred years or so on either side of a central point, so that in most European and Asiatic cultures for any objects later than about 3000 B.C., the archaeologist can usually give a more exact date than the scientist. For objects from earlier periods, into the dating of which a good deal of guess-work has hitherto necessarily entered, a date with a margin of 200 years or so is very useful. Owing to technical limitations only certain materials can be used, the best being carbonised wood or other burnt organic matter.

III

Fields of Archaeological Work

THE FOREGOING chapters will have suggested something of the great diversity of studies in time, place and approach which can come within the province of the archaeologist. The subject is today so vast that no one can cover all aspects, even in one country alone. Therefore a beginner in archaeology must decide in which direction his or her interest lies. Narrow specialisation without a background of more general knowledge is not desirable, but at the same time anyone who wants to do useful work must confine his or her activities within a reasonable compass.

It is perhaps easiest to discuss geographical divisions first, with the proviso that the earlier the period under consideration the less important and limiting do these become, until for the Palaeolithic period the student may be expected to cover whole continents in his researches.

The broad geographical divisions within which archaeologists in this country mainly work are European, Mediterranean, Near Eastern, Middle and Far Eastern. Work of of course also carried out on the archaeology of Africa, Australasia and America, but comparatively few people in this country concentrate on these subjects, and they can therefore be dismissed more briefly.

These geographical divisions are however too broad to form workable units. An archaeologist ought to have a general knowledge of and interest in at least one of these areas, though he may and probably can only have a detailed knowledge about a particular country within that area and of a particular period of the history of that country. Moreover, the divisions are not hard and fast; political or economic factors affected their boundaries; so that a student of Roman archaeology may be concerned with places as far apart as Britain and Syria, of Hellenistic archaeology with places from southern France to India, and for Palaeolithic archaeology he may travel to China or South Africa.

Therefore, as workable units we may take European Palaeolithic and Mesolithic archaeology, with the Palaeolithic of Asia and Africa pretty closely attached; the subsequent European Prehistoric period; Europe in the period of the Roman Empire, with of course a background knowledge of Italy itself and the rest of the Roman Empire; Europe in the Dark Ages (or Migration period); Europe in the Mediaeval period; pre-classical Mediterranean archaeology; classical archaeology; Near Eastern prehistoric archaeology; the archaeology of the Near East in the historic era down to the Hellenistic period; Indian archaeology; Chinese archaeology. In the subsequent paragraphs these subdivisions are individually described, and the kind of archaeology which is involved is indicated.

European Palaeolithic and Mesolithic Archaeology. The meaning of the term Palaeolithic period is described in Chapter II. From this description it will be clear that the archaeology of the period is closely connected with geology, both from the fact that the chronology of the period is based on geological evidence, and from the fact that many of the remains are found in geological deposits. Much of the field-work of palaeolithic archaeologists is devoted to the collection of stone implements from gravel beds or other deposits laid down in the Pleistocene period by the various changes brought about by the different glaciations, and to the identification of the geological significance of these deposits. Sometimes animal bones are associated with the implements, and their identification helps to establish the type of climate (glacial or interglacial) of the period in question. Archaeologists concerned with this period must therefore have training in the identification of such bones.

Excavation does not play such a large part in the field-work of the Palaeolithic period as in that of later periods. The geological deposits in which Palaeolithic implements are found are usually too thick and deep to be excavated by archaeologists. Normally, the finds are disclosed in the course of commercial gravel working, and it is only rarely that the archaeologist has the good fortune of being able to extricate objects from their original position. More often they have to be salvaged as deposits are being removed wholesale. As has already been said, the only kind of place where Palaeolithic remains are likely to be found *in situ* is in caves, and these of course can be excavated, though often under rather uncomfortable conditions and in almost inaccessible positions.

The principal study of the Palaeolithic archaeologist must be the typology of the stone implements. He is deprived of much of the information about the men of the period such as is available to those working on later stages by the fact that most of his finds have been removed from their original position by geological action, and are rarely found associated with others in a group. Thus, most of the information about the cultural groups of the periods must be based on similarities or divergencies in the manufacture of their stone implements, the only surviving artifacts. The student of the period must therefore be thoroughly conversant with different techniques of stone-working, and be able to assign his finds to the various cultures from the evidence of their shape and the technique of their manufacture.

The Mesolithic period is usually grouped with the Palaeolithic as a subject of study. But though a knowledge of the typology of the stone implements is still an important part of the student's equipment, there are many differences in the study of the two periods. These principally arise from the fact that the Mesolithic stage comes after the end of the Ice Age, and thus after the great geological changes of the Pleistocene period. Therefore the remains left by Mesolithic man can often be found *in situ* in the place in which he lived. For this reason, excavation plays a greater part in the archaeology of this than of the preceding period. Mesolithic habitation sites can be excavated, and the finds studied as an associated group.

One of the most interesting aspects of the archaeology of the Mesolithic period is man's adaptation of himself to the changing climatic conditions of the immediate post-glacial period. The study of his natural environment is therefore of importance for this, and also for establishing the chronology of a group, for the various climatic phases of the post-glacial period can be broadly fixed. Some deductions as to the environment can be made from the associated animal remains, or the remains of fish and shell-fish. But still more can be done from the identification of the contemporary vegetation. Mesolithic sites are often in low-lying positions and may be associated with deposits of peat. In the peat can be preserved the pollen of the contemporary vegetation. A study of proportions of the pollen from different types of trees will show the kind of forest in existence and thus the climate. For example a preponderance of pollen grains of oak and elm is evidence of a warm, moist climate, and one of pine and birch is evidence of a dry, cold climate, at least in winter.

An archaeologist working on the Mesolithic period must therefore have a knowledge of the natural sciences, such as botany. He need not himself be able to identify the pollen grains, but he must understand the methods sufficiently to be able to take the requisite samples, and to use the reports of the specialists to elucidate archaeological problems. Again, though he may apply to an expert for the detailed examination of the bones found, he should be able to recognise the more common specimens, and to understand the implications of the presence of the different animals.

European Prehistory. There is naturally no rigid division between the archaeology of the Mesolithic and the succeeding Neolithic period, for the men of the earlier stage were not blotted out, to be succeeded by completely new races. But the beginning of the Neolithic stage marks a very important step forward in the road towards civilisation, and the material remains of the period are correspondingly more complicated. To the archaeologist perhaps the most salient fact is that the use of domestic pottery becomes common (occurrences in a few Mesolithic sites are claimed but not universally accepted; even if they may be, such sites are rare). To a study of the typology of the stone implements the archaeologist must thus add a study of the typology of the pot forms, which becomes increasingly important in later periods as the range of forms becomes greater and more complex.

As is described in Chapter II, the Neolithic stage is marked by the introduction of agriculture and stockbreeding. Men are no longer wandering hunters, but tend to settle down to comparatively sedentary life in larger communities than was possible in the food gathering stage. Therefore, the remains left behind are much more substantial than those left by the huts occupied for a season by a group of Mesolithic hunters. It follows that the opportunities of identifying and excavating a settlement of the period are much increased, and from this stage on excavation plays an ever greater part in the archaeology of the different periods.

Nevertheless, the Neolithic inhabitants of Europe were simple folk, though those classed as Neolithic in the Near East were starting to develop into comparatively highly organised communities. Excavation of a Neolithic site in Europe involves the tracing of huts made mostly of wood, turf and earth, forming perishable structures which require (as will be seen in Chapter V) skilled and patient excavating. In Britain the more easily identifiable sites are those associated with characteristic camps, in which the enclosing ditch consists of a series of unconnected quarry-pits, from which material was derived for a continuous rampart.

But still more easily identified than any of the occupation sites are the burial mounds. The European Neolithic peoples buried their dead in great communal tomb-chambers beneath mounds of earth or stone, usually a long oval in shape. Very few of these have survived intact, but a detailed examination of the structure will often reveal something of the ceremonial attached to the burial rites, and also affinities with makers of similar mounds elsewhere. Thus to the study of the typology of implements and pottery, a study of structural typology is now added.

In Chapter II, reference is made to the spread from the Near East to Europe of the ideas and discoveries which brought about the Neolithic revolution. That we now know that this is so is because it has been possible to connect up link by link peoples in the two areas, by similarities in their pottery, implements and buildings. Thus the Neolithic peoples of Britain can be shown to have arrived by different routes, of which the most important are up the Atlantic coast of Europe and across France, by comparing remains in this country with remains on the continent. The archaeologist dealing with this period has therefore to pay great attention to the distributional aspect of his finds and their typological connections.

In dealing with the Neolithic period, the archaeologist is somewhat less dependent on help from the natural sciences than in dealing with the earlier periods. Nevertheless, he cannot present a true picture if he ignores the natural environment, and this is true of all the subsequent periods. Animal bones, turf layers and so on must be observed and recorded, and he must know when to call in an expert to report on the animal remains or on how a particular layer of soil was formed.

In many ways the problems of the archaeologist in studying the European Bronze Age are similar to those of the Neolithic period, since the European communities are still quite simple. A study of the evolution of the different bronze tools and weapons of course forms an important part of the subject. The great development of trade, which, as we have seen, is stimulated by the use of a metal only found in certain areas, adds the tracing of trade routes to the subjects on which the archaeologist may hope to find evidence, while the tracing of cultural connections is again important for showing the movements of populations.

In Britain the period is differentiated from the earlier by the fact that very few occupation sites are known. This is because the inhabitants of at any rate the earlier part of this period were mainly, owing to a change of climate to drier conditions since the Neolithic period, comparatively nomadic pastoralists. They therefore did not occupy any one place for any length of time and thus left few traces of occupation behind. By far the greater part of the finds of the period come from burials, which at the beginning of the period are mostly under circular mounds (as contrasted with the long barrows which are typically Neolithic) and in the Late Bronze Age are in urnfields, that is to say, cremation burials enclosed in burial urns and set, usually in groups, in the ground. Most of the excavation of Bronze Age remains therefore consists of investigating the burial mounds. The most interesting part of this work is the deductions which can be made about the ceremonial associated with their construction, deductions which can be made if the excavation is skilful enough to reveal all traces of wood and turf structures or of trodden surfaces.

In the Late Bronze Age the use of metal tools and weapons increased very greatly. A study of the typology of the products of the bronze industry therefore becomes increasingly important. Finds sometimes include hoards of implements, the stock of a travelling bronzesmith, which were either accidentally lost or were buried in times of peril. In Britain we begin to find farmstead sites belonging to some of the new groups arriving from the continent, who, as the climate gradually changed again and became more moist, were able to settle down as farming communities.

The Iron Age in Europe is marked by great population movements in central Europe, as powerful groups acquired new and improved weapons in the new metal. These weapons helped them to attack their neighbours, while the rich cultures they developed were copied by their less advanced contemporaries. To these cultures increasingly important contributions were made by the civilisations of the Mediterranean area. These movements, both warlike and cultural, in central Europe, set up a chain of reactions in the outer fringes, including Britain, and movements of populations or spreads of culture introduced new elements all over Europe.

The tracing of these movements therefore forms a large part of the study of the European Iron Age. The material remains available to archaeologists become increasingly numerous. Many more settlement sites appear, while population movements and pressure on land made it necessary in many areas to have fortified sites as a refuge in time of trouble, or even occupied permanently.

A study of this period therefore offers the archaeologist considerably more scope for excavation than does that of earlier periods. From the excavation of the hill forts and settlements he can obtain information as to how the inhabitants lived, their methods of fortification and how these were modified by the introduction of new weapons, their agricultural economy, their trade and their

1 & 2. (above) Excavating with trowel and hand shovel. (below) Section showing foundation-trench of wall cutting earlier levels, Jewry Wall, Leicester.

3. Trench-built and free-built foundation.

cultural connections. The evidence produced by excavations forms material for study of many different sorts. Fortification methods, tools and weapons, pottery, brooches and other ornaments; evidence of agriculture from traces of fields, from methods of storing corn and from farm implements; of stock breeding from animal bones; and, towards the end of the period, coins, all form subjects which must be studied by the excavator or by experts whom he consults.

The artistic achievements of Iron Age man in Europe are far more important than those of his predecessors, excepting perhaps those of Upper Palaeolithic man. In the second phase of the Iron Age, the La Tène period, there is a rich development of an art which combines inborn Celtic inspiration with motives and a stimulus acquired from the Mediterranean and even Eastern civilisations. This creative ability produced remarkable works of art in many parts of Europe, including Britain, and thus art history and appreciation may become part of the work of the archaeologist or his associates.

The foregoing paragraphs will have shown that, though we have taken European prehistory from the Neolithic to the Iron Age as one of the main workable units for the study of archaeology, there are different characteristics in the different phases. The student would in due course probably concentrate on one of these phases, and even on one country within that phase, according to his interest in subject or method. He should however have a broad knowledge of all the phases in order to be able to appreciate truly the significance of the subject on which he is concentrating.

Europe in the period of the Roman Empire. The study of Roman antiquities is one of the subjects which earliest attracted the interest of antiquaries, and classical archaeology was the first branch of archaeological work in which university teaching was provided. It developed, in part, directly out of the study of classical literature and history. The archaeology of the whole Roman Empire is of course closely interconnected, but since the remoter provinces contributed less to literature and art than the Mediterranean and thus

formed a minor part of the old-established studies, and since in each
of the provinces the underlying native culture plays an important
part side by side with the Romanising influences, the approach to
the archaeology of Britain and the other provinces has been rather
different from that to the older subjects of classical archaeology.
The archaeology of Roman Europe thus falls into place in a description of the archaeology of Europe in other periods, while classical
archaeology will be discussed later.

As has just been said, the pre-existing native cultures made considerable contributions to the life of the various European countries
during the Roman period. Nevertheless, the archaeologist is con-
fronted with a new situation when he comes to the Roman period.
Britain and the rest of north-western Europe (excluding its more
outlying parts) come for the first time within the scope of written
records, which began some three thousand years earlier in the Near
East. For the preceding periods in these areas, archaeology alone is
available to build up the story of events, with the exception of a
few slight references in classical sources. In the period of the Roman
Empire, the story is told by a combination of written sources and
archaeology. Nevertheless, the contribution of archaeology is still
very important. Roman historians were naturally more interested
in events in Rome than in outlying provinces. We learn something
about the provinces when a historian is describing the course of a
war, particularly when he is interested in the achievements of an
individual general, as Tacitus was interested in those of his father-
in-law Agricola. But even when such accounts exist, they are often
scanty and inaccurate, and for times of peace or for areas not
concerned with wars we have little written information, and we
must then rely on archaeology. A comparison of a history of Roman
Britain written in the nineteenth century with one written today will
show how much scientific archaeology can add to history.

An archaeologist dealing with Roman Britain or the other Roman
provinces will obviously have to acqruie a basic knowledge of
Roman history, organisation and culture. Features such as military
organisation and structures, roads, town planning, public buildings,
coinage and the like are much the same over wide areas of the

Empire, if not the whole. The student must therefore know something of these subjects in their wider setting, and be able to interpret what he finds in their light. He must also know the history of, and literary references to, his area. At this period architecture first becomes important in north-west Europe. It is true that most of what is found in provinces such as Britain is of modest architectural pretensions. But nevertheless remains are occasionally found of buildings which are related to more grandiose buildings elsewhere in the Empire, and the student must know how to interpret them. A knowledge of general structural problems is also desirable.

Roman Europe offers great opportunities for excavation, and more of this has perhaps been done in Britain than any other part of the Roman Empire. Excavating on a Romano-British site is possibly the best training a beginner can get. The structural remains are usually substantial and the levels well-defined, while the problems involved require careful working out. A student well-grounded in such work can easily adapt himself to the more elusive structures of other periods, or the more complex problems of eastern archaeology.

There are many different types of sites of the Roman period to be tackled by excavation. In the first place there are the military sites. These range from great legionary fortresses such as Lincoln and Chester, through smaller forts such as Seguntium above Caernarvon and Margidunum in Nottinghamshire and the late Saxon shore forts such as Burgh Castle in Norfolk and Pevensey in Sussex, to small signal stations on the Yorkshire coast. The fortresses and earlier forts conform to general rules of military planning, and from comparatively scanty remains the exact use of structures can often be determined. The history of these military sites as revealed by excavation is of great importance as evidence for the Roman frontier policy and concerning times of war and danger. A special branch of the subject is the study of the defences of northern Britain. The Hadrianic Wall from the Tyne to the Solway has been the subject of meticulous examination, and year by year new information is produced about its component parts. The Antonine Wall from the Clyde to the Firth of Forth has also been closely examined. Recently, however, air photography has revealed many new military sites in this frontier area, and there is plenty of work to be done to learn its full history.

Most of England, however, formed part of the civil zone of Roman Britain, and work on the civil sites therefore bulks larger than that on the military sites. The Romans greatly encouraged town life, and many of our towns owe their origin to Roman rule. They of course vary greatly in size, from Roman London of 330 acres and Verulamium of 200 acres, down to Alchester of 26 acres and they varied also in status and character. London always had a special status, given by its position at the lowest place where it was possible to bridge the Thames, and for most of the Roman period it was probably the administrative centre. To it were thus brought officials from other parts of the Empire and foreign traders. Verulamium also had a special status as a *municipium*. Four cities, Colchester, Gloucester, Lincoln and York, were *coloniae*, where time-expired army veterans were settled, and of which the population would therefore include foreigners from other parts of the Empire who had served in Britain. The rest of the towns were, however, country towns of various degrees of size and importance, inhabited for the most part by Romanised Britons.

The excavation of such towns has thus much to tell us about the civilisation and organisation of Roman Britain. We can trace the stages by which the inhabitants became Romanised, the rise and decline of their prosperity, we can find the evidence of trade and industry, and such information is very important for building up the general history of the province. Conditions of excavation vary greatly. A few Roman towns lie beneath fields, for instance Verulamium and Viroconium (Wroxeter). The greater number have modern towns on top of them, and Londinium and Camulodunum can only be recovered in fragments beneath modern London and Colchester. The archaeologist thus may be working in pleasant fields or within the confines of a modern cellar on a site which is about to be rebuilt.

The other principal type of civil site is the villa, a country house which may be a simple farmhouse or an elaborate mansion with

fine mosaic floors. These are the centres from which the greater
part of the country was farmed, and associated with the villa (which
often has a subsidiary bath block) there may be farm buildings of
various sorts: barns, granaries, threshing floors, corn-drying ovens,
labourers' quarters. The examination and dating of the complete
layout of these complexes gives us important information as to the
economy of the countryside. Great numbers of villas have been
investigated from time to time, but unfortunately very few fully or
scientifically, and much remains to be done before we have a clear
picture.

The inhabitants of the villas, even of the smaller ones, were
Britons who had acquired a substantial degree of Romanisation and
who farmed their lands in an up-to-date manner. Side by side with
them, though mostly in different areas, we find peasants living in
isolated homesteads or groups of huts, whose way of life, even
towards the end of the Roman period, differed little from their
Iron Age ancestors. They farmed in the same primitive way and
lived in very similar huts, but bought objects which they did not
make themselves, like pottery, in the local Romanised market-town,
and for these transactions used Roman coins. The excavation of such
sites is therefore very similar to that of an Iron Age site, but the
different structures can be dated by the finds to the Roman period.

Various other sides of life in Roman Britain can be investigated
by excavation. Pottery kilns are encountered in many parts of the
country, and a study of the distribution of the wares from individual
kilns provides interesting evidence about trade. Tile factories are also
found. As well as temples within the towns, a considerable number
have been found in isolated parts of the country, sometimes with
elaborate complexes of associated buildings. Iron working in the
Weald, lead, copper and other mines, provide evidence of industry.

A study of great interest is that of Roman roads. Many of the
great main roads, in Britain as in the rest of north-west Europe,
owe their origins to Roman engineering. Their planning in a series
of straight stretches is known to everyone, and renders them readily
identifiable on a modern map. Some sections, however, went out
of use at an early date, and it needs painstaking research to recover

them. Such research may include the consideration of topographical features which may have determined their line, examination of old records in which they may have served as landmarks, spotting of straight lines of hedgerows, and finally probing or excavating on a suspected line to confirm a hypothesis.[1]

There are therefore many fields open to the excavator of Roman Britain. But the finds of the period are so numerous and diverse that there are also many fields of study available for those who do not themselves want to excavate. Coins, inscriptions, pottery—especially the closely datable Terra Sigillata or Samian ware imported from Gaul and Germany—architecture, mosaics, are all specialist studies, of which the results contribute to those obtained from excavation or field survey.

Europe in the Dark Ages or Migration Period. With the break up of the Roman Empire and the incursion of barbarian tribes into its area, most of north-west Europe loses for the time its close contact with the civilised world and thus with written history. Therefore we are once more largely dependent on archaeology for evidence as to the course of events. This is particularly true of Britain, where Roman civilisation was almost completely submerged in the barbarism of the incoming Anglo-Saxon tribes, while in Gaul there was more continuity and the newcomers absorbed more Roman culture.

In Britain, Romanised urban life almost entirely disappeared, though the process was a gradual one about which archaeology is beginning to teach us something. The early Saxons and other tribes lived in primitive structures which are difficult to locate and about which we have so far not much evidence. Problems of excavating them are very similar to those of excavating Iron Age settlements. Most of our information comes from burials. A study of the burial urns and the associated objects such as brooches and other jewellery has been able to assign different types to different groups of invaders. A comparison of these objects with similar ones found on the continent has shown the place of origin of the different groups,

[1] See Bibliography.

while a study of their distribution in this country enables the course of the invasions to be worked out.

In dealing with the earlier part of this period, therefore, excavation of occupied sites plays a much smaller part in archaeological investigation than in the two preceding periods. Cemeteries have to be excavated as they are found, which is usually accidentally for there are generally no surface indications, but that is rather a different matter.

The barbarian invasions only affected what was to become England, leaving the rest of the British Isles to the Celts, and in Wales traces of sub-Roman civilisation were long preserved. In particular, the Christian Church in Wales, Ireland and southern Scotland maintained contact with the Church on the continent. A certain amount of archaeological work has been done on sites of this Celtic fringe, but as yet evidence is scanty. The written records of some of these Celtic Christians have survived from the sixth century onwards, and throw a few glimmerings of light on what was happening.

The first century after the end of Roman rule in Britain is 'dark' in a very real sense, from the almost complete absence of written records. Gradually, however, as the Anglo-Saxons became organised into more settled groups, written records begin to be available again. The archaeologist of the period must thus be in close touch with historical and linguistic studies and be able to use their evidence to interpret his own. The study of place names is a branch of linguistic studies which can be of great help to archaeologists as evidence of the spread of the invading groups.

Europe in the Mediaeval Period. The transition from the Dark Ages to the Mediaeval period is a gradual one, taking place at different times in different countries. In fact, there is no dark age in the Mediterranean area, where Byzantium carried the tradition of Rome straight on into the middle ages, and where the barbarian tribes rapidly came under the influence of Roman civilisation. In more outlying parts of Europe, particularly in Britain, the process was much slower.

In the Mediaeval period, archaeology plays a subsidiary part to history, for we now begin to get the national records of the different European countries, as opposed to references in Roman records, and the national record is naturally a fuller one. Nevertheless, archaeology has still a contribution to make in illustrating everyday life as opposed to the history of kingdoms.

For this period too excavation is perhaps subsidiary to other aspects. This is partly due to the fact that a number of public buildings survive above ground level. Excavation may be necessary to recover wooden structures associated with an early Norman motte, or to complete the plan of a ruined castle. There may be earlier phases beneath extant churches, or monastic buildings associated with an abbey may have disappeared. For such studies, excavation is necessary, but may often form part of the study of a visible building.

The archaeologist dealing with the Mediaeval period must thus have a knowledge of the architecture of the type of building, castle or church, with which he is dealing, and a knowledge of architectural history to be able to date the structures and fragments he finds.

Another reason why excavation is subsidiary is that so often Mediaeval towns and villages lie beneath modern successors. Mediaeval structures, other than public buildings, are usually of slight construction, and have often been obliterated by the modern buildings. All that remain may be pits and wells, which sometimes can be excavated when a modern building has been destroyed.

An exception to this general rule is the case of a Mediaeval village which was abandoned completely, usually as the result of the Black Death or other catastrophe. A beginning is being made in the excavation of such villages, and much interesting information is to be expected as to everyday life and country economy. It is however a fact that the technique of field archaeology as evolved in other branches is only gradually coming to be applied to Mediaeval remains, since much could be learnt without it. It is now being realised that such techniques can greatly increase the possibilities of exact knowledge, and questions of pottery chronology and so on are now being carefully studied.

For the Mediaeval period there are of course many subjects cognate to archaeology on which a student who is not primarily interested in structures or excavating can concentrate. These include subjects such as art and sculpture, history of arms and armour, numismatics, glass, jewellery, ceramics, and many others. The subject therefore provides a variety to suit all tastes.

Pre-classical Mediterranean Archaeology. Pre-classical Mediterranean archaeology is concerned particularly with the archaeology of Crete, of the Greek mainland and islands prior to the classical Greek period, of Malta, Sicily and Cyprus, and to some extent of the lands fringing the Mediterranean. It thus includes a study of one of the great civilisations of the Near East, and it has connections both with Near Eastern and with European archaeology.

For the story of the Minoan Empire of Crete we are entirely dependent on archaeology, since the decipherment of Minoan and early Aegean scripts is still in its early stages. The great excavations of Sir Arthur Evans have provided material for the working out of a detailed chronology of the Minoan civilisation from the third millenium B.C., contacts with Egypt and other Near Eastern countries having provided a framework into which the successive stages revealed by excavation can be fitted.

Excavation has therefore played the most important part in Cretan archaeology. This has been supplemented by a very detailed analysis of the finds. Since work in Crete has always been very closely allied to that in Greece, the methods of stylistic analysis of pottery decoration, wall-paintings and so on have been applied very successfully to the Minoan material. A student wishing to take up Cretan archaeology must therefore be trained both in excavation and in such stylistic methods.

The relations between the Minoan and the other great Near Eastern civilisations are very important in the history of the ancient world. A student must therefore have a broad knowledge of history and modern archaeological work affecting these areas.

Though the importance of Crete tends to dwarf that of the rest of the area with which we are concerned, the whole forms an important link in the spread of progress from the Near East to Europe which is described in Chapter II. Particularly for the Neolithic and Bronze Ages, a study of these phases, and their links on the one hand with Anatolia and the rest of the Near East, and on the other with central and western Europe, is most important. A comparison of finds and structures in Anatolia, Crete, Malta, Italy and the Balkans has helped to establish the routes followed by the spread of cultures to Europe from the Neolithic period onwards. Much new and scientific work on this subject remains to be done, particularly since much of the material which archaeologists have had to use has been unscientifically excavated.

At the end of the Bronze Age and in the Iron Age the centre of interest shifts to mainland Greece. Incursions of barbarian tribes from the north broke up the Minoan Empire, as also other Near Eastern civilisations, and introduced new elements. This is the stage reflected in the Homeric legends, and archaeology is gradually showing the setting to which these legends refer. Out of these elements was evolved the classical Greek civilisation, which began the shift of the centre of progress from the east to the west. Excavation and the comparative analysis of finds have still a big part to play in the archaeology of this period.

Much work has been done on the archaeology of Cyprus. From its position, the island inevitably has close links both with the mainland to the east and north, and also with the other Mediterranean islands to the west. The archaeology of the island has thus its contributions to make to the study of this area, but for most of its history Cyprus seems to have been the recipient of influences rather than an originator of them, and care must be taken in applying Cypriot chronology to mainland cultures.

Almost all the material for the archaeology of the Mediterranean in the pre-classical period must be produced by excavation. But past finds have been on a great scale, and there is therefore also plenty of scope for anyone who prefers to work on the finds provided by excavation, and to become an authority on pottery, art, seals and other classes of objects.

Classical Archaeology. It has already been pointed out that classical archaeology is the oldest established branch of the subject. It dates from the days in which rich patrons of learning were acquiring from the Mediterranean masterpieces of great sculpture and when the education of young men of fashion was completed by a grand tour which might include visits to famous Greek and Roman sites.

The foundations of classical archaeology were thus established in the study of objects or buildings for their own sake. Moreover, literary sources provided the historical, chronological and cultural background against which such things could be studied. It follows that classical archaeology has been much less dependent on scientific excavation than the newer branches, and has concentrated more on stylistic studies. Comparatively recently, excavations have begun to add to the facts available for these stylistic studies by providing chronological evidence for developments, and have also brought to light new information about the history of sites.

The classical archaeologist is concerned with the study of the products of classical Greece, its descendant the Hellenistic Empire, and its successor the Roman Empire, though as a rule any one individual archaeologist tends to specialise in one or other of these subjects. Closely linked to this aspect of archaeology is the study of the subject in the areas of the Mediterranean provinces of the Roman Empire. Here Roman culture, rooted in many cases in a Hellenistic past, is much closer to that of Rome than is the case in the northern provinces. The work of the classical archaeologist is therefore centred on Athens or Rome, and he may also from these centres broaden his field to include the products of the great Hellenistic or Roman cities such as Alexandria in Egypt, Antioch in Syria or Lepcis in Tripolitania.

A classical archaeologist must therefore be equipped with a sound knowledge of ancient history and literature. If he is to work in the field, he must have training in classical architecture and planning, and he must have a thorough knowledge of the pottery. But owing to the bulk of material already in museums, and of buildings already uncovered, there is much scope for those who do not wish to excavate. Sculpture, architecture, art as demonstrated in wall-paintings and mosaics, pottery, numismatics, are all subjects in which detailed studies are carried out unconnected with excavation, though of course excavators are also often experts in many of these subjects. But the number of those concerned primarily with the museum side of the subject will probably always be higher in this branch, proportionately to the excavators, than in any other.

The excavator of a classical site has many advantages over those dealing with other periods. He is less likely to bring exciting new facts or cultures to light, but he has the chance of dealing with buildings or objects of first-class artistic or architectural merit. He has a knowledge of what he is likely to find, for the buildings and planning for the most part follow established principles, and he has much comparative material to help him to elucidate what he finds. This means that he has to have a good knowledge of such comparative material as a background. On the other hand, the sites often have a long history, covering many building phases, and the excavation is therefore complicated and requires high technical skill.

Not all countries will allow foreigners to work in their area. The extent to which foreign expeditions are welcomed varies somewhat with political conditions, and the following notes, applicable in 1960, may require revision from time to time. Work is now possible in Greece and the Greek islands after a period of difficulty following the war. Italy is now prepared to admit foreign expeditions, which was not the case before the war. Foreign expeditions are welcomed in the new state of Libya, comprising the former Italian North African possessions. The successor states to Palestine, Jordan and Israel, both welcome foreign expeditions. Permission can in theory be obtained for work in Egypt, but there are many restrictions. Foreign expeditions are now allowed to work again in Syria. The Turkish authorities now admit foreign expeditions, not allowed before the war, and there are a number of first-class sites in Asia Minor on which work is needed.

The Archaeology of the Prehistoric Near East. The study of the earliest cultures of the Near Eastern area is one of very great importance. The amount of Palaeolithic material so far discovered is not very great, but is of considerable interest. Anyone undertaking this work must of course be trained in the Palaeolithic of Europe. For the succeeding phases, however, studies in this area are differentiated from those of Europe, though very important for their understanding.

It has been described in Chapter II how the great revolutions and discoveries in the Near East were the beginning of the progress of mankind towards civilisation. Since the end of the Second World War, there has been a great increase of knowledge of, and interest in, the evidence for the first development of settlements and agriculture, developments which are now seen to stretch back to at least the seventh millennium. There is still much to be done to make the picture clear, and to establish the date of the developments in the different areas, but excavations are gradually providing evidence for the different stages, the earlier perhaps in Palestine, Syria, and Northern Iraq, followed by developments in the river villages of Mesopotamia and Egypt, where the next step forward to urban development took place.

From the evidence of such excavations the early history of these areas has gradually been deduced. The artifacts of different groups have been identified, and thus connections between individual settlements established. As far back as the fourth millennium B.C., contacts began to be developed between distant groups, even between Egypt and Mesopotamia, and therefore rough synchronisms can be worked out.

For this branch of archaeology, therefore, excavation is of primary importance, for it alone produces the necessary evidence. The excavator's problems are similar to those involved in examining any prehistoric site. He has to establish the cultural affinities of the people with whom he is concerned, for which pottery provides some of the most important evidence. He has to establish their way of life, their social and economic organisation, their relations with their neighbours, their natural environment. For this he must have the necessary skill in excavation, and knowledge of how to interpret his finds and the reports of experts on technical and natural scientific matters. He must also have a good knowledge of the contemporary cultures of other parts of the ancient world.

The broad framework of development in the prehistoric Near East has been established by work of this sort in recent years, but there are still many gaps to be filled. In particular, the prehistory of Anatolia is only gradually being worked out, while a mere beginning has been made in that of Iran. Something is known of connections with the Mediterranean area and with Europe, but very little so far about connections with the countries to the east.

The Archaeology of the Historic Near East. In the third millennium B.C. the Near East starts to emerge into the era of history with the beginning of written records. As the organisation of the communities with which he is dealing becomes more complex, so the work of the archaeologist becomes more complicated. As with European archaeology, we in due course reach the stage where specialisation is necessary, and no one can be an expert in all the different branches of knowledge.

The progress of development in different areas varied greatly. Thus in, or just before, the third millennium we get the foundation of the Old Empire in Egypt, culminating in the Pyramid Age with its elaborate political and religious organisation and established method of chronology and records. In the valleys of the Tigris and Euphrates the various city states are in turn securing hegemony over their neighbours, and we have the evidence of great riches and high art of the Royal Tombs at Ur. But during the same period most of the peoples of Palestine and Syria were living in small and primitive communities, and only gradually acquiring the use of bronze.

The great and specialised developments in Egypt and Mesopotamia, and the great differences in culture in other countries makes it almost inevitable that even when dealing with this period the archaeologist must concentrate on one area, though it is most important that he should be acquainted with the results of research in other areas. Also the complication of excavation technique on the one hand, and the wealth of epigraphical material now accumulating on the other, means that it is almost impossible for one person to be master of both aspects. The position is very different from that of the classical archaeologist, who may be expected to have studied the languages, very modern and comprehensible compared with the ancient oriental languages, from his school days onwards. In dealing with the Near East the archaeologist and the linguistic scholar should each know enough about the other's work to be able to appreciate its importance, and to use its results, but cannot themselves be expected to have more than a superficial knowledge of each other's techniques.

The principal subdivisions of Near Eastern archaeology in the historic period are Egyptian, Mesopotamian, Anatolian, and Palestinian and Syrian. Each of these is such a very large subject that it is unusual for any one archaeologist to be an authority on all aspects.

The wealth of finds from Egyptian sites is well-known to any visitor to national museums all over the world. Excavations were carried on in Egypt throughout the nineteenth century, with the result that we now have a comparatively full knowledge of the Old Empire in the first two thirds of the third millennium, of the Middle Empire in the beginning of the second millennium and of the New Empire in the second half of that millennium, and rather less information about the intervening and succeeding periods of disturbance. Much of this knowledge comes from tombs and religious structures, but secular buildings have also been excavated.

There is, nevertheless, still scope for discoveries, particularly about the earlier periods and about the less spectacular buildings. For many years, however, excavation in Egypt has been hindered by regulations refusing the excavator any share of the finds, with the inevitable result that foreign museums are not prepared to finance expeditions. Promises made in 1959 in connection with the salvaging of antiquities endangered by the Aswan Dam may give hope of a more liberal policy, with the result that field-work in Egypt may be stimulated.

There is, in any case, much material for research in finds already available. Egyptology is one of those branches of archaeology in which the museum side of the subject plays a larger part than present-day fieldwork. Epigraphic studies form a very large part of it, and there are many works of art and other objects which still require study.

The position of Mesopotamian archaeology is not unlike that of Egyptian, in that a great mass of material was found in the nineteenth century, when finds illustrating the great buildings and works of art of the First Dynasty of Babylon at the beginning of the second millennium, and the later Empires of Assyria and Babylonia, were made in rich profusion. The twentieth century has, however, added greatly to our knowledge of the subject, and carried back the story into the third millennium, the period of the different city states, of which the most famous is Ur. Excavation is still producing very important new discoveries, including a wealth of epigraphical material, and our knowledge of exact chronology, of religion and of art is steadily progressing and being extended backwards in time.

But though excavation today in Mesopotamia plays a larger part than it does in Egypt, museum work is as important as it is in Egyptology, since there is a similar wealth of material. For those interested in the linguistic side, there are great numbers of cuneiform tablets already discovered which still await study, and there is always work to be done on the seals, the weapons and other small objects as well as large works of art.

The archaeology of Anatolia is a comparatively new subject, since for long excavation there was difficult. Gradually, however, knowledge is accumulating about the great periods of Hittite rule, which have so many contacts with the Empires of Egypt and Mesopotamia. Now evidence is being produced about the earlier periods, but there is still much to be done, and there is no doubt that this is one of the most fruitful fields for future study.

The archaeology of coastal Syria and Palestine form in reality one subject, for the division is a comparatively modern one. They have tended to be treated separately since the Biblical associations, of Palestine attracted to it an attention in the nineteenth century which was not given to Syria, while the fact that after the first Great War Syria became a French Mandate and Palestine a British one has resulted in work in Syria being mainly carried out by the French, while Britons have concentrated on Palestine.

4. Post-hole and sleeper beam of wooden wall (in front of the stone wall).

5 & 6. (above) Foundation of wattle-and-daub wall with post and single line of wattling. (below) Foundation of wattle-and-daub wall with multiple stakes.

Neither area has the same intrinsic importance in the ancient world as have the other areas just mentioned. But since they formed the connecting route between these other areas, their history is of importance to all of them and helps to throw light on their relations. The history of Palestine, moreover, has the great interest of its connection with three of the great religions of the world. Archaeology has shown the background of small Semitic states against which the Israelite religion and culture was formed. The general picture is by now fairly clear, but there is much detail yet to be filled in, and there is no doubt that the excavation of sites which will throw light on Biblical research will always attract much interest.

Inland Syria forms a rather different province from the coastal area, since its connections with Mesopotamia and Anatolia are very close. Its archaeology has always been closely associated with that of these countries, particularly with Mesopotamia. The area was important particularly in the second millennium, when the civilisation of the more advanced river valleys began to spread to it, and states, such as that of Mitanni, grew up there to rival the older empires.

Thus excavation forms a most important part of the archaeology of Syria and Palestine. The objects found are not comparable in intrinsic merit with those of Egypt and Mesopotamia, and therefore the museum side of the work is rather less important. Nevertheless, the close connections of the area with adjoining empires places great importance on comparative work on the finds. Fairly recent discoveries of epigraphic material, especially at Ras Shamra, have emphasized the contribution which Semitic texts can make to the study of religion, and textual work is a very important side of the work, as is also the study of all the objects and buildings which throw light on religion.

Towards the end of the first millennium B.C., the new Mediterranean civilisations begin to exert a reverse influence on the Near East. From the Hellenistic period onwards, most of the area comes within the orbit of the classical world, and forms one of the most readily accessible areas for the classical archaeologist. Both classical and Byzantine archaeology here are subjects of which there is still much material and many sites requiring study.

Yet another branch of Near Eastern archaeology is that of the Moslem remains. Hitherto, this has mostly been concentrated on architecture and art, for much is still extant above ground. Some work is, however, now being carried out on buried remains, and the recent excavation of an early Arab palace at Khirbet Mefjah in Palestine has shown what remarkable results may be produced from excavation. Overlapping in period with the Moslem remains are those of the Crusader period, which again have mainly been studied from the fine structures, especially castles, still visible above ground.

Indian Archaeology. Indian archaeology is in itself an enormous subject, for quite apart from the Palaeolithic remains, its prehistoric civilisations go back to at least the third millennium B.C., while there are naturally many varieties of contemporary cultures in the great sub-continent. The study of Indian archaeology has tended to be divided into two main fields, the prehistoric, with most attention paid to the great Indus Valley civilisation dating from the third millennium B.C., and work on the art and literature of the much later Hindu, Buddhist and Moslem cultures of the present era.

The discovery of the Indus Valley civilisation with the great cities of Mohenjodaro and Harappa has been one of the most outstanding developments of twentieth-century archaeology. We now know that the Indus Valley had a civilisation comparable with the early ones of the valleys of the Nile and Tigris and Euphrates, and there is sufficient evidence of trade between India and Mesopotamia to show that it was flourishing at about the same time. We know less about it for not only has much less work been done on it, but also we lack decipherable written records.

There is thus much work to be done on this subject, chiefly in the way of excavation to get a fuller picture of the towns and the extent of the culture. There is also a tremendous amount to be done to link up this civilisation with that of Mesopotamia, for the intervening area is almost unknown and there is need of both surveys and the excavation of selected sites.

Knowledge of the period between the decay of the Indus Valley civilisation and the historic era has only very recently begun to be put on a sound basis. The difficulty is to relate the different groups of cultures known in isolation in different parts of the country, and to tie them down chronologically, for the contacts with the fixed chronology of the Near East are very scanty. Recently, brilliant use has been made of contacts with the Roman world through trade in the first century A.D. A series of carefully chosen investigations has linked the culture so dated with others right up the sub-continent, and thus a beginning has been made in providing a framework.

This is a beginning only, and a great deal of work remains to be done before all the known material is put in its place, while there is no doubt much that is quite unknown. Prehistoric Indian archaeology, in addition perhaps to that of Anatolia, is probably the field which offers the greatest promise of new discoveries and in which there is the greatest need for scientific and carefully planned work. Much of the basic work must be the survey of sites and the recording of their surface remains, accompanied by excavation of key sites.

The other branch of Indian archaeology, the study of Hindu, Buddhist and Moslem cultures, has mainly concentrated on the artistic, historical and epigraphic aspects. Here again, the amount of material is very great, and there is much scope for those interested in the museum approach to archaeology.

Chinese Archaeology. This is perhaps the branch of archaeology in which, at any rate for Europeans, excavation has played the least part. Most of the very fine specimens in western museums have been acquired as collector's pieces. The various stages of Chinese civilisation are comparatively firmly established, and the work of the archaeologist is mainly concerned with art history and technique. The principal subjects studied are those of painting, sculpture, ceramics and language, and the beauty of the objects offers a great attraction to students. The comparatively few excavations have established that behind the historic civilisations is a long prehistoric development, and there is no doubt that much work could be done in this field if conditions were favourable.

Other Branches of Archaeology. Almost every area in which the archaeology is studied leads on to others, either linking up with another field which is well known, or fringed by areas as yet largely unknown. Western European archaeology links up with Russian, hardly known to most archaeologists outside Russia, and the Asiatic area beyond, as well as with the Near East. Egyptology connects with that of the Sudan and the more primitive regions beyond. Mesopotamian archaeology is closely connected, at least in the early stages, with that of Iran and the other hill countries to the east, and via Baluchistan with India. India is, of course, connected with the other countries of east and south-east Asia on the one hand, and with Afghanistan and the Asiatic hinterland to the north. Thus, associated with every comparatively well-known sphere there are other little-known ones. These provide scope for those who wish to branch into the unknown, and who are prepared to face the difficulties of exploration in out-of-the-way parts. Some of these areas may today be blocked by insuperable political difficulties, but there are plenty which are not. But though exploration in such areas may mean that quite new subjects may be opened up, it does not mean that those undertaking it may nowadays start from scratch as regards archaeological knowledge. They must be thoroughly grounded in archaeological technique and in knowledge of the cultures of the areas adjacent to those in which they are planning to work.

Mention was made in the beginning of the chapter of African and Australian archaeology. This is the study of comparatively primitive societies. Their cultures have connections with the Palaeolithic stage of Europe, and the methods involved in their investigation are those of the palaeolithic, and also those of ethnology and anthropology, for they merge into the study of present day tribes. Work in Australia and South Africa is naturally carried out mainly by people resident in those countries but in the African colonies there is a need, which is receiving growing recognition, for British archaeologists to devote attention to the subject.

Another subject mentioned at the beginning of the chapter was that of American or New World archaeology. Many people are attracted by the romance of the great Inca and Maya civilisations which preceded the European contacts with America, and by accounts of ruined cities standing amidst the jungle. In America considerable work has been done on these civilisations, but at present in this country there is no training available, though our national collections are rich in objects from them. Work is also being carried out in America on the ancient culture of the American Indians and the other primitive groups of the continent. Such studies, like the Australian and African archaeology, are closely linked with anthropology. In Appendix II are given details of the training in this subject in American universities, where, naturally, most work in this branch is being done. Tuition in some of its aspects is, however, provided at Oxford and Cambridge, where the University museums house large collections of relevant material.

Though this chapter has been a long one, the outline given of the different fields of archaeology has necesasrily been very brief. The only intention has been to sketch the principal characteristics of each field in order to aid the beginner in a decision as to which field of study to embark upon. It may be repeated that there must be no suggestion that archaeologists should be narrow specialists. They should have an understanding of the general course of development in other areas, a more detailed one of the areas adjacent to their own, but must as a rule concentrate most of their energies on one main field. There is much to be said, however, for making a start on British archaeology, both because it is close at hand and can be started on at an early age, as will be seen, and because the basic principles can be much better learnt, both in field work and in theory, than when dealing with the vast sites and problems of eastern countries.

IV

How to Become an Archaeologist

THERE IS NO ONE answer to the question of how to become an
archaeologist. People have embarked on archaeology in many
different ways. In the past it has certainly been a very haphazard
affair. A man who was a professor of classics or ancient history or
divinity might feel the urge to learn more of the towns of Greece
or Palestine, and set out to dig one up without any more ado, and
with no strictly archaeological training at all. One of the greatest
British archaeologists, General Pitt-Rivers, was a regular soldier
who developed an interest in the typology of fire-arms. He happened
to succeed to a large estate on the borders of Wiltshire and Dorset
which was very rich in ancient remains, and then turned his methodi-
cal training as a soldier and his interest in typology to devising
scientific methods of investigating these remains. In so doing he
became the father of modern archaeological technique in Britain.

Nowadays, however, the standards of scientific archaeology, both
in field work and in the analysis of finds, have been so firmly
established that no one ought to undertake work on his own without learning from the experience of his predecessors, that is to say
without being trained. He must study the results of past work so
that he knows the background in his selected field, and he must
learn the methods evolved by past experience. It is because the
subject has become so complex, with such a huge accumulation of
knowledge already acquired, that university training courses have
been greatly multiplied in recent years.

But this is most emphatically not to say that only those who have
taken a full academic training in archaeology can do good work in it.
Comparatively recent developments have brought about the creation
of a number of full time posts, whose holders can devote all their

54

attention to archaeology, and who can thus be called professional archaeologists. But the subject has grown up on an amateur basis, through the labours of people to whom it was a hobby or a part-time occupation, and it will always be largely dependent on them. It is most unlikely, and most undesirable, that there will ever be enough full-time archaeologists to do all the work.

Nevertheless, it is useful to talk about professionals and amateurs, without being in any way derogatory to the latter, as it is inevitable that they should set about becoming archaeologists in different ways. The former should aim at obtaining a full-time concentrated training while the latter will have to train for his own career and acquire his archaeological training in a more piecemeal manner.

Youthful Beginners. Many prospective archaeologists develop an interest in the subject at a comparatively early age, as schoolboys or schoolgirls, and the question then arises as to how they can get to know something about it. The most obvious way is to join some society which arranges talks, expeditions and perhaps excavations. Some beginners are lucky enough to have school archaeological societies which they can join, and this is actually the best beginning. The average local or county archaeological society is not always suitable for schoolboys or schoolgirls, as the interests of such societies are often too recondite, but some have junior sections which are very useful. The first interest of young beginners is usually in excavations, and it ought always to be possible to arrange for them to help on a dig, though it may not always be possible to find one within reach of their homes, which may be a difficulty. Schoolboys or girls can do most useful work on digs, and all excavators ought to welcome them both for this and because it is so important to encourage possible future recruits. So the first thing to do is to make enquiries about what excavations are available. As a first step, enquiries should be made from the local archaeological society, and if no help can be obtained here, application should be made to the Secretary of the Council for British Archaeology. (See Appendix V.)

Other youthful archaeologists are interested in collecting objects of antiquity. There are two words of warning about this: to avoid collecting shams and to avoid destroying important archaeological evidence. For both reasons you must get the help of an expert. You can learn about the objects in which you are interested in museums, and you should, if possible, get someone who knows about them to explain them to you. Then, to avoid destroying archaeological evidence, you should always report any finds you make. If you find an area with a lot of Roman or prehistoric pottery, or with many flint implements, you should make sure, through the local museum or archaeological society, that the area is already known. If it is not, arrangements can then be made for it to be recorded.

Archaeology as a Profession.   Many people in whom an interest in archaeology is aroused will want to make it their profession, and the question then arises as to the possibility of making a living in it. The answer has to be given with some caution. As has already been said, there are now a number of full-time jobs in archaeology. But this number is still restricted in comparison to those in many professions. The result is that there are usually a considerable number of candidates for all good posts, and, because of the fact that vacancies only occur rather sporadically, it may be necessary to wait for a time, after training is completed, before a vacancy occurs. Therefore, anyone who is completely dependent on his earnings must consider the matter seriously and decide whether he is prepared to take the risk. Many, who are quite clear that archaeology is the only subject in which they are interested, will be prepared to do so. Others may feel that they cannot do this, and will prefer to take some training which will give them a second string to their bow. But though this paragraph has emphasized the gloomy side, it is fairly safe to say that anyone who shows real ability will in due course get a suitable job, though there may be a difficult period at first.

The full-time posts available fall into three main categories: University, Civil Service, and Museum.[1] There are now quite a considerable number of departments of archaeology in various British universities. Between them they cover all the main branches

[1] A summary of the various posts, and of methods of application for them, is given in Appendix IV.

of archaeology described in Chapter III, though it must of course be realised that there are more departments in some branches than others. Classical archaeology for instance, is well provided for, while Chinese archaeology is taught at only a few universities. The chances of obtaining a university post must vary accordingly.

The Civil Service departments which have archaeological appointments are the Ancient Monuments Inspectorate of the Ministry of Works, the Royal Commissions on Historical Monuments, and the Archaeology Section of the Ordnance Survey. Appointments at the national museums also come under the Civil Service, but they are included in the next paragraph. The Ancient Monuments Inspectorate is charged with the care of the monuments and historic buildings for which the Ministry of Works is responsible. Much of such work is concerned with the maintenance of the structure of buildings, and their restoration where necessary, and with the preservation of prehistoric monuments such as hill-forts or barrows. Occasionally the Ministry carries out excavations of sites which are in its custody. The Inspectorate also advises on questions of scheduling Ancient Monuments, and if a scheduled Ancient Monument has to be destroyed or damaged, arranges for prior excavation. The Historical Monuments Commissions for England, Scotland and Wales are responsible for completing scientific field-records of all monuments down to 1714 and selected monuments to 1850. This is carried out county by county, and in fact amounts to writing the prehistory and history of the county in the light of its monuments. The staff is therefore concerned with making the detailed record county by county. The Archaeology Branch of the Ordnance Survey, of which the staff is small, is responsible for the archaeological information which appears on the Ordnance Survey maps, and for preparing the special archaeological maps which appear from time to time. The work thus involves accumulating exact information as to the find-sites of archaeological objects, and the supervision of the planning and identification of ancient sites.

The most numerous class of archaeological posts is that of museum curators and assistants. It requires but little knowledge of museums in Britain to realise that these vary very greatly. The big national museums have many departments, including all branches of archaeology. The majority of the larger civic or county museums mostly have separate departments of archaeology with full-time archaeologists in charge. Many of the smaller museums, however, have one man in charge of several departments or the whole museum, and though his primary interest may be archaeology, he will have to acquire a knowledge of zoology, geology and other subjects. The larger museums may be concerned with the archaeology of many parts of the world, whereas the smaller ones will be mainly concerned with local British archaeology. The work of assistants or curators in the different types of museum will vary accordingly. Those in the national museums will be concerned, in addition to dealing with matters of museum display, with questions of research in the province of their department. Those in local museums will be concerned with research in local archaeology and with the recording of local finds. They may have the opportunity of excavating local sites, which may indeed be a duty if such sites are threatened with destruction. They also have the extremely important job of arousing the interest of the general public in local history. In addition to the assistants and curators, a number of museums have posts for archaeological technicians who are concerned with the treatment of archaeological finds.

It will be noticed that though excavation is involved in connection with some of the posts just discussed, in none of them is it the only job. There are in fact no paid full-time excavation posts. Almost all digs in Britain are seasonal affairs. While the dig is in progress, the director and the senior assistants may get some pay, even though it is usually only a subsistence allowance. But for the intervening periods there is no pay, even though work on the finds often has to be carried out during them. Excavations in the Near East are naturally longer term affairs, during which the assistants may be paid. A very few such digs have in the past had a permanent staff employed for a number of years, but even such posts are temporary in the sense that any one dig is of limited duration.

In connection with museums, mention has been made of archaeological technicians. This is a branch of archaeology in which an increasing number of full-time posts are becoming available, principally in museums, but a few also in universities and Government departments. The term may be used to cover specialists in the treatment of archaeological objects, draughtsmen and photographers. The treatment of archaeological objects covers a wide range of subjects from the repair and restoration of pottery to elaborate chemical treatment of decayed metal and other objects. Nearly all finds from excavations require such treatment, and many of the larger museums now have trained technicians on their staffs for the purpose, while the smaller ones send their materials to central museums or the research departments of universities. The Ministry of Works also has a small department dealing with this subject. There are therefore a number of appointments for trained persons, though, as is the case with other types of archaeological posts, vacancies may only occur sporadically. Some of the larger archaeological expeditions, especially those working overseas, also employ specialists in the treatment of objects, to mend pottery, to assist in extricating fragile objects from the soil, and to give first aid treatment to them. But as with all posts in connection with excavations, employment is on a temporary basis.

There is a very considerable demand for first-class archaeological draughtsmen. They are employed mainly on the drawing for publication of objects from excavations, and the making of fair copies of plans and other drawings for the same purpose. In some cases they also undertake the surveys and plans of sites in the process of excavation. There are probably not very many full-time posts for such draughtsmen. A few museums and universities have appointments, while the Ancient Monuments Inspectorate and the Historical Monuments Commission employ fairly large staffs. But there is plenty of opening for free-lance draughtsmen, and anyone whose work is of high quality would quickly get a sufficient connection in the archaeological world either to make a full-time job of it, or to supplement other work. If, for instance, someone who wished to make archaeology his career were also a good draughtsman, he could easily tide over an interval before obtaining an appointment.

There are also openings for persons specialising in archaeological photography. The basis of qualification is of course technical skill in photography, but the particular problems of photographing archaeological sites and objects do require a specialised knowledge. Most posts are in connection with museums, though only the larger museums can offer such appointments. Again there are, however, a few university and Civil Service posts. Most of the larger excavations employ a specialist photographer, and more should do so, but again such employment is only temporary.

Training for Prospective Professional Archaeologists. The basic training for a prospective archaeologist is a university degree. (The question of the training of archaeological technicians is somewhat different, and is discussed below.) To have a chance of obtaining almost any of the posts described above, it is nearly essential to have a degree, and this is likely to become increasingly the case.

The subject in which a degree is taken will depend both on the university selected and on the branch of archaeology in which the candidate is interested. At many universities archaeology is considered too specialised a subject to form the sole study for a first degree. It is either taken as one subject with others, or as a postgraduate course. The last method clearly gives the most thorough training. A synopsis of the methods adopted by the various universities is given in Appendix II. There is actually much to be said for taking archaeology as a postgraduate study. Not only is a wider subject a better general education and of more cultural value, but a degree in, for instance, classics or history, is a qualification in a much wider field. Should the interests of the person concerned change, or should he find it difficult to obtain an archaeological post, he then has his general degree qualification to fall back on in following some other career.

Someone proposing to attend one of the universities at which archaeology is not a principal degree subject will have to consider what he is to read. It is not essential that he should take a subject directly connected with his proposed future work in archaeology, for in any case he benefits from the training involved in working for a degree. But most people will tend to take a subject which leads fairly directly to their future career. If this is the case, they must decide which of the various fields of archaeology described in Chapter III interests them most. In the case of some fields, the choice of a degree subject is obvious. Someone intending to study classical archaeology will clearly read classics, as will someone intending to work on the allied field of provincial Roman archaeology, for instance, Roman Britain. Probably, too, the best preliminary study for someone proposing to concentrate on the preclassical archaeology of the Mediterranean is also classics, though if Greek and Latin do not appeal to him, it would be possible to approach it from the side of history. Oriental languages are an obvious approach for a prospective student of Near Eastern archaeology, but again if studies of language do not appeal, or are found difficult, history could be chosen.

For some branches, especially European prehistory, there is no closely allied general subject, and indeed this applies to the prehistory of all regions. Those hoping to go on to study such a subject must choose their degree subject for its general educational value and training in method. Probably the best two such subjects are classics and history, for besides their intrinsic merits, they both teach the kind of approach which will be required. Other possible subjects would be geography or anthropology.

The degree course having been completed, more detailed training in archaeology should be acquired. It should be noted, however, that such additional training is not an absolutely essential qualification for obtaining one of the jobs described above. A candidate might be accepted on the strength of his degree and expected to get training in archaeology in the course of his job. Additional training in archaeology is of course a useful extra qualification for an applicant and enables the holder of a post to settle down there quickly to original work.

Details of such additional training vary in the different universities; an outline will be found in Appendix II. In general, it consists of a course covering the present state of knowledge of the subject selected, that is to say, the history of the countries concerned in the light of archaeological evidence, and details of such evidence. If the civilisation was a literate one, training may include the language and literature. In addition, it should include practical archaeology, that is to say an introduction to excavation technique, surveying, draughtsmanship, photography and the treatment of finds. Even if the candidate's interests are not primarily in field work, he should receive this training, for he will probably be largely dependent on the results of field work in his studies, and he should be able to assess the value of the evidence with which he is dealing.

Pre-University Training. Schoolboys or schoolgirls who have decided to make archaeology their career often ask for guidance as to the best subjects to study while still at school, particularly after they have taken their School Certificates. This will of course depend partly on what they are going to read at the university and partly on what branch of archaeology they wish subsequently to study. Subjects connected with their future degree work will be obvious, and no advice on that is needed here. As to other subjects, probably the most generally useful one is ancient history, if that can be arranged. Whatever the field of archaeology subsequently to be studied, it is almost sure to overlap chronologically with, and to have contacts with, the classical world, to the history of which most ancient history courses are limited. A knowledge of classical ancient history is therefore a useful background, and there is also much to be said for a continued study of Latin (and Greek if the candidate is good at ancient languages) as contributing further to this background. A reading knowledge of modern languages, especially French and German, is essential to an archaeologist, as he will have to read books and periodicals in these languages to get the material for his work, and these could usefully be studied while still at school. Geography and economics might be helpful accessory subjects.

In the way of direct archaeological training, the most useful thing to do is to work on excavations in the holidays. This not only introduces the beginner to field work, but he hears archaeological matters discussed and meets senior archaeologists. It is of course important that he should get this experience under skilled guidance,

and not that of someone who has no training in scientific archaeology. If he does not know anyone who can advise him in this
matter, he could get in touch either with the archaeological department of the university to which he is going, or with the Council
for British Archaeology. (See Appendix V.)

Training for Amateur Archaeologists. I have explained above (p. 55)
that I have used the terms professional and amateur to distinguish
between those holding a full-time archaeological post, and able to
devote their whole time to archaeology, and those whose career is
in some other field and who can therefore only give their spare time
to the subject. In the context of this chapter such a distinction is
necessary, for clearly only those hoping to obtain an archaeological
post will take full-time training in the subject. There may still be
some people who can afford to work full-time on archaeological
subjects without obtaining a paid post, but in modern conditions
these are few and far between, and need no special consideration
here, for they can be included among the professionals.

But in the archaeological world the distinction between professional and amateur is little used, for much first-class work is done
by men and women whose paid occupation is in other spheres, and
they rank as experts equally with those whose career is archaeology.
One of the greatest experts on Gaulish Terra Sigillata in recent
years was a doctor of medicine, another was an Admiralty clerk;
another doctor is a well-known excavator and authority on ancient
systems of agriculture. One can hardly think of any career offering
less leisure than that of doctor, but these two managed to find
time to become leading authorities.

Therefore, no one who for any reason feels that he cannot make a
career of archaeology need think that he cannot do useful work in the
subject, and he should set about getting as much training and experience as time will allow. There are three main ways in which this can
be done—attending lectures, reading and helping on excavations.

Opportunities for attending lectures of course depend on the
locality. Lectures may include both university lectures and those of
archaeological societies. It may be possible to attend a course of

lectures in archaeology at a university in which one is reading another subject. Some universities, for instance London, admit persons who are not taking a specific examination to attend courses. In this way a thorough training can be obtained, particularly if spread over several years. But either in addition to this or as a substitute for it, a prospective archaeologist should join one or more archaeological societies, a national one which deals with the branch of the subject in which he is interested, and a local one if he has local affiliations. The lectures of the national societies are mainly held in London, but many of these are subsequently published in their journals. The programmes of these societies probably cover matters of wider interest than do those of the local society, but it is important that a prospective archaeologist should belong to local societies. By so doing he will meet other people interested in the same subject; through the local society he may get the chance of first helping on, and then being responsible for, excavations; finally, local archaeological societies are the backbone of British archaeology, and everyone interested in the subject should support them.

The books on archaeological subjects are by now legion. A bibliography of the most useful works for a beginner is given in Appendix I. In addition to them there are a number of important periodicals. The majority of these are published by archaeological societies for their members. Other useful ones are given in Appendix I. Such periodicals contain much of the latest archaeological material, including excavation reports. A beginner in archaeology will gradually learn a great deal by studying them.

Many part-time archaeologists start their training by helping as volunteers on excavations. Such training is necessarily limited to British archaeology, for part-timers cannot as a rule spare the time to take part in excavations overseas. It is fairly safe to say that nowadays most directors of excavations in Britain are prepared to welcome untrained volunteers, and to give them training, though naturally they are still more welcome if they have been able to obtain some preliminary theoretical training by reading or attending lectures.

The section on European archaeology in Chapter III will have given a would-be archaeologist some help in making up his mind as to the period which interests him most, and will thus help him to select a dig he would like to join. If he wants to assist on an excavation in his own locality, the local archaeological society will probably be able to tell him what is available. If he wants to go farther afield, he should apply to the Council for British Archaeology for information. It is not as a rule fair to the director of an excavation to offer to come for less than a fortnight, since in a shorter period the director would not get much help in return for the training he is giving.

Normally, beginners are expected to give their services voluntarily, for funds at the disposal of most excavation committees do not cover more than the expenses of navvy labour for heavy work (where such is necessary), the overhead expenses of tools, stationery and so on, besides the inevitable sequel of publication expenses. A few of the bigger digs do make subsistence grants to some volunteers, but they can seldom afford to do so to many, and naturally such grants are given in preference to those who have had some experience. Such assistance may take the form of grants towards cost of living, or a payment per hour of work.

The personal qualities expected of a volunteer on a dig are that he, or she, for women are just as welcome as men, should be reasonably active and strong, not afraid of hard work, prepared to assist in everything from plodding through apparently uninteresting levels to washing and marking finds (though most directors are kind enough not to give a volunteer dull jobs for too long) and above all he or she must not be afraid of getting dirty. Even in fine weather, excavating is dirty work, and in wet weather can be indescribably so.

The work of volunteers is mainly the careful excavation of archaeological levels, usually with a small tool such as a trowel. If a thick and unproductive level has to be removed with pick and shovel, most directors prefer to use a professional navvy if they can afford to employ one, as they do such work so very much better than someone not trained to use these tools. Sometimes volunteers may be asked to do pick and shovel work, and many in fact enjoy it, but no one need be deterred from offering to help on most digs by the fact that they feel that pick and shovel work would be too heavy for them, since there is almost always plenty of other kinds of work.

There may be some people who would like to help on excavations without doing actual digging, and in most cases they will be very welcome. On many digs, especially Roman and Iron Age, there is much work to be done with the finds, as will be described in more detail in Chapter VII. Pottery and bones have to be washed, marked and packed up. Finds have to be indexed and sometimes given elementary first aid. If there is someone who is willing to undertake such work, it is a great help, as it enables other volunteers, who would otherwise have to do it, to spend more time on actual digging. Other non-digging assistants who are very welcome are people qualified to undertake the surveying or photography, but their work must of course be of a high standard, and they must be prepared to learn the specialities of the archaeological type of work.

The equipment with which a volunteer who is going to dig should arrive on a site is simple. The principal requisite is old clothes which can be allowed to get dirty without a qualm. Strong shoes are necessary in most seasons, though in fine weather sandals or plimsols may be all right. Gum-boots are a great help, for even in fine seasons morning dew may be quite enough to soak one's feet. An old mackintosh is essential, for one can never count on not needing one either for rain or cold. Beginners are strongly advised to provide themselves with a pair of old leather gloves, unless they are already pretty horny-handed, as working with a trowel can easily produce blisters at first. Most expeditions provide the actual digging tools, though some volunteers prefer to have their own trowel, a 5-inch or 6-inch pointing trowel. A useful accessory is also a rubber kneeling mat such as gardeners use, as there are seldom enough on a dig to go round.

So far I have dealt with the training of part-time archaeologists. Some people will never want, or have time, to do more than help on excavations in their holidays. Others will want to go further and to become experts. As the examples given at the beginning of this section show, this may either be as excavators or as specialists in particular subjects. Excavating will develop naturally out of assisting as a volunteer on a dig. Those who are keen and show promise will be given more responsibility, and in due course may be asked to take charge on an excavation of their own. Both senior assistants and those in charge of excavations may expect to receive some pay, though it will rarely be more than a subsistence allowance to cover their out-of-pocket expenses. Those who wish to become expert in a particular aspect, who may or may not be also excavators, will in the first place be guided by their own interests as to the field they select. Within that field, they can easily get advice as to the particular subject in which specialisation would be useful, for instance a particular kind of pottery, the typology and distribution of a particular class of weapon, implement or monument, and so on. There are many subjects in which there is plenty of scope for detailed study, and archaeologists are always glad to know of specialists to whom they can refer for reports on their finds. Such work is as a rule voluntary.

Finally, part time archaeologists can do much valuable work in field surveys of various sorts. This branch of archaeology is described in Chapter VIII. Similarly, they can be of much assistance if they make it their business to keep under observation all sites in their neighbourhood which are likely to produce antiquities, gravel pits producing Palaeolithic remains, housing sites which may cut into ancient settlements, cliff falls which may reveal prehistoric pits, in fact any disturbances of the soil. They will want of course to make themselves familiar with the type of object or remains of occupation likely to be found in their neighbourhood, which they can do by reading or attending lectures. They must also make arrangements for recording their finds, which is usually best done through the local museum or local archaeological society. They must know enough about the subject to realise if a find is of real importance, and whether steps ought to be taken to have a site excavated before it is destroyed. This can best be done either again by the local museum or local society, if these have the necessary experts available, or else direct by the Ancient Monuments Inspectorate of the Ministry of Works.

V

The Technique of Field Work: Excavating

No ATTEMPT HAS been made in the earlier chapters of this book
to provide anything in the way of a manual of instruction, for each
of the fields of archaeology described in Chapter III would require
a manual to itself. All that has been attempted is to give guidance
to someone about to take up the subject. This chapter goes somewhat beyond the earlier ones in that it aims at giving actual technical
instruction. It deals with a technique which is common to all fields,
instead of with a volume of knowledge from past work which would
be required in a manual covering any of the fields of archaeology.
There is still a great lack of books dealing with excavation technique, and it is a help to directors of excavations if new volunteers
have some knowledge of the principles and procedure involved.

But it must be very strongly emphasized that reading is no
substitute for experience in excavation, only an adjunct to it.
Nothing can teach a beginner the feel and look of layers of soil,
on the interpretation of which all excavation results depend, except
practice. No one should therefore attempt a dig on his own until
he has worked, probably several seasons, under a competent
excavator—not, in fact, until he has been told by persons under
whom he has worked that he is sufficiently experienced to do so.

It must be remembered that all excavation is destruction. The
evidence concerning an ancient site is contained in the layers of soil
comprising its floors, and those which lie above and beneath them.
Once these layers have been disturbed, the evidence is disturbed,
and has been destroyed altogether unless it has been properly
observed, recorded and subsequently made public. Therefore, unless
the person doing the excavation is properly equipped to do so, it is
much better that the site should be left untouched.

Principles of Interpretation.   The science of excavation is dependent
on the interpretation of the stratification of a site, that is to say the
layers of soil associated with it. The term stratification is also used
by geologists with reference to the layers which go to make up the
crust of the earth, but in archaeology we are concerned only with
those layers, extremely recent geologically, which have accumulated
during or since man's occupation of the particular site. Some of
these layers may have been actually made by man, for instance a
layer of rubbish above a hut floor, or the actual floor itself; others
may have been made by natural processes, for instance a layer of
wind-blown sand over an Eastern village or a layer of humus over
deserted site in the west. In any case its significance has to be
interpreted. The term stratification may also be applied in the
archaeological sense to things which are not strictly layers at all,
but pits, banks, trenches, in fact any disturbance of the soil.

People who have not worked on excavations usually do not
realise how very varied are the different layers which make up the
soil on a site where there has been lengthy human occupation. Each
surface that was walked on for any length of time, each layer of
debris, each tip line in a bank, shows up as a distinct line in the soil
if it is looked at in the side of a cutting. Moreover, it is almost
impossible to disturb the soil by, for instance, digging a pit, cutting
a ditch or driving in a post, without leaving evidence which enables
the trained excavator to interpret what has happened. Each such
pit or ditch cuts through the pre-existing layers of soil, and even if
the same soil is filled back into the cutting, the layers are broken,
and these breaks are visible in the side of a cutting and usually
horizontally at the bottom of the excavation as well. As will be
seen, it is on the interpretation of these layers and disturbances that
depends the elucidation of the history of the site.

In order to be able to recognise layers and their significance as
one digs them, one must understand how they were laid down. Very
primitive communities may live in the open or in very slight huts
or in caves, and therefore all that would be found on sites occupied
by them would be a layer of their rubbish, including objects they
have used, overlying whatever soil existed when they arrived there,

and sealed by later layers which had accumulated by natural or human agencies at a later date. But in most cases of human occupation of a site there are the remains of the structures in which the inhabitants lived. In such sites there is a logical sequence of events, the evidence of which ought to be recognisable.

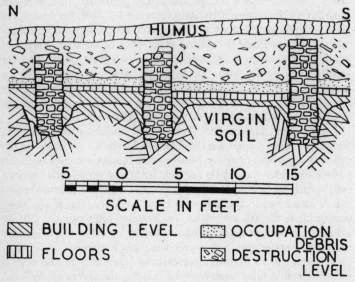

Fig. 1. Section through masonry structure of one period only.

The simplest instance is that of a structure which is established on a virgin site, has a comparatively short life without undergoing any alterations, is then destroyed or decays, and is in due course covered by vegetation and humus. In that case, one would find the following layers from the bottom up (Fig. 1): pre-existing virgin soil; building level; floor of beaten earth or some more solid surface; occupation debris; destruction level; humus which has accumulated subsequently, owing to the growth of vegetation.

If the site has never been previously occupied, the soil on which it is built will contain no human relics. The building level will consist of the soil disturbed by the builders of the structure. It may be no more than the puddling and levelling of the pre-existing soil. It may consist of soil disturbed to sink substantial foundations, or imported to level an uneven site. From an archaeological point of view, its importance lies in the fact that it may contain objects of human manufacture, for it is a layer deposited by human action. These objects may include something which was lying about on the surface, or something brought in with a load of soil to level up, and they may of course be of any date prior to the construction of the building. But the building layers may also contain things dropped by the builders, the fragments of the jar which contained their lunch, or some coins out of their pockets. Such finds may therefore help to establish the date of the construction of the building. It must of course be remembered that the objects may have been in use for some considerable time before they were lost. The jar may be an old one, though if it is of common ware it is not likely to be *very* old. The coins may have been in circulation for a considerable time; if one looks at one's small change today, one may find a coin of 1860 or even earlier, though the proportion of later coins will be much higher, and therefore the chance of dropping one of these will be proportionately greater. But at any rate there will obviously be nothing later than the latest ones minted at the time. Therefore, the date of the building will be at least as late as the latest object in the building layer, and sealed by the floor, while it may be appreciably later. If the excavation methods are such that any possible disturbances subsequent to the erection of the building have been eliminated, as will be described below, one can thus establish the earliest possible date at which the structure was put up, though with objects less closely datable than coins, for instance prehistoric pottery, the margin may be a fairly wide one.

The occupation debris will contain the objects lost or broken during the use of the structure. The extent to which such debris exists will depend on the type of culture with which one is dealing. The floor of a prehistoric hut was obviously a pretty messy affair.

Debris of meals was left lying about, broken pots and lost ornaments were trodden into the dirt on the floor, and such a layer, which is easily recognisable from its contents and consistency, would be very representative of the culture and period of the occupants of the hut. The mosaic floor of a Roman house, on the other hand, would probably be kept clean until the house was destroyed or fell into decay. But in this case one may be fortunate enough to find a rubbish pit which one can associate with the occupation of the house, and its contents would provide similar evidence. The objects recovered from such layers or pits would be roughly contemporary with the occupation of the structure, again with the proviso that some may have been old when lost.

The contents of the overlying destruction level will depend somewhat on what was the final fate of the structure. If it was abandoned and left to decay, the inhabitants would probably have taken away their current possessions, and the finds may not be particularly informative. If, on the other hand, it was destroyed by fire or other catastrophe, it would include, mixed up with the debris of the destroyed structure, the equipment of the house at the time of the destruction. The houses of Pompeii, for instance, had in them, when excavated, the household pottery in use at the time of the eruption. This pottery therefore can be dated to the year A.D. 79, the historical date of the eruption, or to the short period before that date which is likely to be covered by the life span of domestic pottery. Most destruction cannot be given a fixed date like this; on the contrary, the date of destruction must be inferred from the date of the objects contained in the destruction layer, in so far as this date can be established from a knowledge of the objects.

Above the destruction layer, in most circumstances, humus will gradually accumulate in temperate climates, while in dry climates wind-blown sand or soil will be deposited. Such layers will not of necessity have any objects of human origin. There may be an occasional object dropped by a passer-by, but unless there is a later settlement in the neighbourhood, such objects will be scanty. It often happens, however, that objects from the destruction level get disturbed and transferred into the humus level. This may be due to traffic, though most usually to agriculture, which may begin after the humus layer has become sufficiently thick to provide enough soil for cultivation. Agricultural operations, particularly ploughing, tend to eat into the layer below the humus and thus add to the thickness of the agricultural soil. Objects thus transferred into the humus level cannot be allowed the significance of those *in situ*, but nevertheless they have a bearing on the length of time a site was occupied.

A site with a sequence such as has just been described is unusually simple and straightforward. It more commonly at least happens that a structure has several phases, which may only mean that floors are relaid, or may mean that the actual structure is added to or altered. The principles of the interpretation of the associated objects and dating evidence is the same, but care must be taken to assign the alterations to the correct phase. It may happen that one structure overlies another of an earlier period. If so, the levels belonging to the earlier structure may be disturbed when the later is put up, and objects from these incorporated in the building level, and these objects must therefore be identified and carefully interpreted. On a Romano-British site, it is quite usual to find a succession of two or more buildings one above the other (Fig. 2), while the extreme example of such a sequence is found in the ancient cities of the Near East, where in the course of centuries one city after another has been built on the ruins of its predecessor (Fig. 6).

A final complication is likely to be disturbances cutting down into underlying deposits. Later occupants may dig pits; for instance, the inhabitant of an Iron Age hut may dig a storage pit, or a modern farmer may dig a pit to bury a sheep. Such pits may introduce objects of a later period into the level of the ancient structure, and, unless the disturbance has been identified, will confuse the evidence.

A very frequent cause of disturbance on a site where there are substantial structures is the removal for re-use of the building stone or brick from the walls (Fig. 2). This may happen at any stage. When a building is abandoned, its walls may immediately be dismantled. Alternatively, it may crumble into ruins, out of which its walls may be subsequently dug. This removal of walls may be only

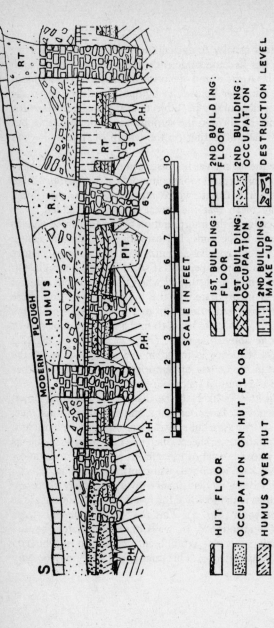

Fig. 2. Section through a site on which the first occupation is represented by a hut with wooden posts. This was succeeded by a period of abandonment, in which humus accumulated. A house was then built, with a metalled road along the south side. This first house was dismantled, its walls being partly robbed to their bases, and was succeeded by a second house. Above the decay of the second house humus accumulated, and the area was eventually ploughed.

SCALE IN FEET

0 1 2 3 4 5 6 7 8 9 10

HUT FLOOR

OCCUPATION ON HUT FLOOR

HUMUS OVER HUT

1ST. BUILDING: FLOOR

1ST BUILDING: OCCUPATION

2ND BUILDING: MAKE-UP

2ND BUILDING: FLOOR

2ND BUILDING: OCCUPATION

DESTRUCTION LEVEL

NATURAL SOIL

to floor level, in which case no great damage is done to the archaeological evidence, for the plan can be recovered from the lines of the
foundations, and the floor levels will be intact. On the other hand,
the robbing may be carried right down into the foundations, sometimes removing them completely. This of course leaves no structure
which can be planned. Also it results, when the robbing has been
completed, in a trench being left along the lines from which the
walls have been dug out. In this trench rubbish gradually accumulates, or may be intentionally filled back, and thus again extraneous
objects may be introduced at or below the level of the floors. The
excavation of such a site, therefore, requires care both to trace the
lines of the walls and to distinguish the disturbed from the intact
levels.

Principles of Excavation. Since the working out of the history of a
site depends on the interpretation of the different layers, it is clear
that the excavation technique must be such that the layers, and the
different disturbances, can be recognised, and that the objects found
can be assigned to the correct layer. The general principles of such
excavation technique are the same when dealing with all types of
site. The application of them varies when working on different
classes of ancient remains, and these varieties of application are
described in the subsequent sections.

The two main principles of excavation are the observation of the
different layers of soil, including any disturbances affecting them,
and the interpretation of their relationship to any structure. Each
layer of soil can be dated only by the objects in it, and it must
therefore be quite certain which layer an object is in, and that the
layer is intact. Secondly, most structures, unless they have an
inscription or are of some quite distinctive style, can only be dated
by reference to the associated levels, and therefore the relationship
must be established beyond doubt. The absolute depth from the
surface of an object means nothing, unless that can be associated
with a defined layer of soil, as can in fact be done by the three-
dimensional method of recording described below. To record an
object as 2 feet below the surface alone means nothing. A floor or

other level may be sloping or the surface may be sloping and the floor horizontal, so that anything at a depth of 2 feet at one end of a cutting will be below it, and at the other above it. Alternatively, at one end it may be in a floor, and at the other in a pit cutting down from the surface.

In most types of soil it is possible to observe the layers as one digs through them. A new layer is indicated by a change of colour, consistency or texture. As soon as there is an indication of a change in the soil, clearance should be carried down to that layer, so that the objects from the upper level can be kept separate from the next one. If there is any doubt as to whether an object comes from the bottom of one level or the top of the one below, it should be considered as belonging to the upper one; an object from an earlier level ascribed to a later one will do much less harm than a later one in an earlier level, for the level is to be dated by the latest object in it. A disturbance such as a pit or robber-trench will show itself as a break in the colour of the soil, by increased softness, or by the inclusion of rubble or debris. The contents of the disturbances must of course be cleared out and finds kept separate from those of the level it cuts. Again if there is any doubt, an object should be assigned to the disturbance rather than to the intact level, as the former is the later deposit. Post-holes of timber structures show up usually as softer and darker patches.

If a wall is encountered, it should be possible to establish as digging is in progress whether the level being dug runs up to the wall or is cut by it. A cut, which will indicate that the foundations of the wall were dug from a higher level, will show as a break in the colour of the soil, or its consistency. If there is any doubt, objects from the soil near the wall should be kept separate until this point has been decided.

But though many of these points will be observed as excavation proceeds, it is essential to be able to check and record them by a visible section in the side of a cutting. In such a section, the layers will as a rule be quite clear. One will be able to see which of the changes in soil observed in digging are significant, and what are their relationship to any structure. Any disturbances, such as pits, will also be visible, and one will be able to see from what layer they cut down.

It is therefore an absolute principle of excavation, which allows of no exceptions at all, that the whole area must not be cleared simultaneously. Standing sections must be left at frequent intervals from the surface down, and it must be possible to relate all structures or disturbances to them. The method of doing this will depend on the type of site being dug, and this will be described in subsequent sections.

The technique of the actual digging is also important. If a professional navvy is set to dig a trench or cutting of any sort, he will automatically do so with a straight vertical edge. This is essential, unless special circumstances require that the side shall be on a batter or slope, as described in the section on digging earthworks. If a vertical face is not kept not only is it much more difficult to read the sections, but the space at the bottom of the cutting becomes much restricted. This making of a vertical face should be done as the digging proceeds downwards, and it is a thing which volunteers find very difficult. The cutting should be looked at from above at frequent intervals, so that any deviation can be corrected. If the sides have to be trimmed down subsequently, there is a risk that it will be impossible to decide from what level objects come, and they will therefore have to be treated as of uncertain provenance.

The excavator must have a straight horizontal line to follow. It is most important both from the look of the excavation and for accurate planning that all cuttings should be laid out accurately. The method of this will again vary with the type of site, and will be described in that context. But in all cases it must be done with a tightly stretched string and not by eye. The excavator can then mark along the line of the string and follow this mark in digging.

A professional navvy in digging will loosen a comparatively small amount of soil, and then clear it up. It is important that volunteers should learn to do this too. If a great deal of soil is loosened at a time, there is a real risk in the first place that some of it will get trodden in again and so confuse the stratification, and secondly that it will not be possible to decide where any object in it came from.

In archaeological digging it is of course necessary to work to the layers of the soil, and this both the professional navvy and the volunteer will have to learn. Ordinarily, the navvy will dig in spits of about four to six inches, according to the consistency of the soil, and will keep a horizontal bottom to the cutting. If there is no change in the soil, this is the correct thing to do. But as soon as any change is observed, work should follow the top of this change, regardless of whether this is horizontal or not. It may sound surprising, but it is better to remove too much than too little, to go a little too deep into the next layer than not to go deep enough. This is because, as has already been said, the attribution of an object from a lower, earlier level to an upper one does less harm than *vice versa*.

The soil must of course be thoroughly examined for objects as it is loosened and cleared away. The thoroughness with which this must be done will vary with the type of site and level. It is waste of time to search the soil minutely if the layer is unimportant, for instance surface soil, or even if it is one in which there is abundant evidence but no rich finds. On the other hand, if evidence from a level is crucial to the elucidation of the history of the site, or if important finds are being made, very great care must be taken that nothing escapes. It should in any event be the rule that no large lumps of soil are thrown up without being broken up, while in the case where great care is needed, the soil must be gone through with the fingers. It is rarely necessary actually to sieve the soil in digging an occupation site, unless very small objects of great importance are being found. It is also rarely possible in Britain since the soil is seldom dry enough to go through a sieve which is fine enough to recover small objects. It may however be necessary in digging tombs.

When the soil has been loosened and examined, it must then be thrown up out of the cutting. According to the type of dig, it may be thrown on to a heap at the side of the cutting, or removed to a spoil heap outside the excavation area. If it is thrown on a heap at the side of the cutting, it must be kept tidy, and well back from the edge of the cutting. It must also be remembered that if one is digging on agricultural land that has got to be restored to use, the top cultivated soil must be kept separate so that it can be replaced on top. The lower levels do not as a rule consist of humus, and are apt to be full of debris, unsuitable for agriculture.

The tools ordinarily used in this country for the removal of upper soil or thick layers are a pick to loosen the soil and a shovel to throw it up. The pick should have one end chisel-shaped and the other pointed. The shovel is broad and slightly curved up at the sides, and is distinct from a spade, which is straight and narrower. Some archaeologists use a fork to loosen the soil, but I have not yet worked on a type of soil on which I should like to use one, and consider that in most hands it is likely, with its multiple points, to do much more harm than a pick. A pick, carefully used, can do extraordinarily delicate work.

For the finer excavation work, a bricklayer's pointing trowel with a five- or six-inch blade is the best implement, or a strong knife can be used. The trowel is used with a scraping motion, and only rarely to dig with the point. For stiffer layers a miniature pick-axe, of the army entrenching tool type, is very useful. With such implements it is easier to follow intricate stratification than with larger implements, and easier to spot objects. It is also easy to clear delicate objects. Soil loosened in this manner may be thrown up with a shovel in the usual way. It is, however, usually more convenient, and essential if working in a confined space, to use a small hand shovel, such as a coal shovel, with which the soil can be cleared into a bucket; this can then be lifted on to the side, or hoisted up to someone above (Pl. 1). Another essential hand tool is a stiff carpet brush, provided the soil is not too wet, to brush a surface clear and generally to tidy up.

Other useful tools on a dig are a mattock, which is a pick with one end axe-shaped, to cut tree roots, a spade to cut turf, or a crescent-shaped turf cutter, which is also useful for trimming the faces of sections, and a stiff broom for general tidying. Special tools for clearing fragile objects, and so on, are dealt with elsewhere.

The principles just described are the basic ones which should govern all excavating. Their application, however, varies on different types of sites. The experienced excavator will be able to adapt and vary his methods according to the needs of the site. In any case, individual experienced archaeologists apply the principles in different ways, which may all produce equally satisfactory results. Therefore, in this section I have no intention of being dogmatic and saying that the way of excavating described is right and other ways wrong. I am simply describing methods which I have personally found satisfactory, as a guide to beginners on how problems can be tackled. But of course when a beginner starts on his first dig, he will have to follow the instructions and methods of the person in charge. He will not be popular if he sets out to correct those under whom he is working. If after a period of work he feels that the methods do not attain a high standard, his remedy is to offer his services elsewhere on another occasion.

The Excavation of Masonry Buildings. The most straightforward type of site to excavate is that of a substantial masonry building of rectilinear plan. Examples of such a site would be Roman and the more solid Mediaeval buildings in this country. On such a site, the succession of structures is not too complicated, the plan reasonably predictable, the structure solid and the depth of deposit not too great. These are the features which enable the methods of excavation to be differentiated from the types of sites dealt with in subsequent sections. There is much to be said for the recommendation that all beginners, whether interested in British prehistory or Near Eastern archaeology, should get their first excavating experience on such a site. On it the principles of excavating can most easily be learnt, and then can be applied on the more difficult types of site to be described later.

In order to be able to interpret the remains of a building as they are excavated, it is necessary to understand how it has been constructed. When any substantial structure is to be built, the first step is to lay firm foundations. These are almost invatiably sunk beneath the pre-existing ground level, since any soil laid down at the time of building would not be sufficiently consolidated to support the foundations. The first step is therefore to dig foundation-trenches along the lines to be followed by the walls. These may be of three

7 & 8. (above) Excavating a barrow, with two segments and the centre cleared. (below) Clearing a site by the grid method.

9. Section through a bank.

main types; a trench wide enough to allow the builders access to
the face of the foundations as they are built; a trench of the same
width as the wall, so that the foundations are laid from above, flush
with the sides of the trench; and a trench which is a combination of
these two methods, the lower part being the width of the wall and
the upper part widening out (Fig. 3).

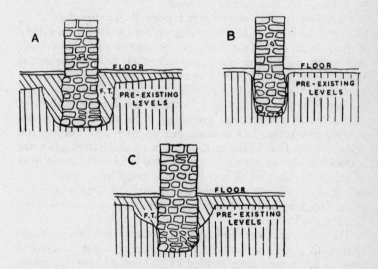

*Fig. 3. A. Foundations built in wide foundation-trench. B. Trench-built
foundations. C. Foundations partly trench-built, partly with wide foundation-
trench.*

In the first case, the resultant foundations will be regular and
the joints of the face will usually be mortared, though the face will
not as a rule be dressed flush, with pointed joints, as it would above
the contemporary ground level. When the foundations have been
laid, the extra width of foundation-trench will be filled in with soil,
probably partly that originally excavated from the trench, but
possibly also including builders' rubbish. When a section is cut

against the wall, this will show, usually quite clearly (Pl. 2). The layers of pre-existing soil will cease short of the wall, and the intervening gap be filled with soil with different layering, often including spreads of mortar from the foundations. The first layer to cross the top of the foundation-trench and run up to the face of the wall will be the contemporary floor and its make-up. Such foundations are described as free-built.

Foundations of the second type are described as trench-built. In this type the face will be much rougher, for the stones are simply laid against the edge of the trench and are often only roughly shaped. Any mortar will be quite rough, and will mainly be in the horizontal joints, being put in from above as each course is laid. There is rarely any difficulty in distinguishing this type of foundation form the last. The foundation-trench in this case will scarcely show in section, but it is often clear, particularly when the foundations are of unsquared stones such as flints, that the lower layers do not run truly up to the face. In any case, the character of the work will make it clear that it could not have been intended to be visible at the level of any of the layers which have been cut through by the foundation-trench. Even if it was not clear from other points, the identification of the floor level will be obvious from the change in character of the work above that point.

The character of the third type of foundation will be a combination of that of the first two (Pl. 3). This is perhaps the most common type, it being the easiest method of building to have the lowest courses trench-built and the upper built free. The identifications of the associated floor level should present no difficulties in this type, for as in the first type there will be a continuous layer crossing a comparatively wide foundation-trench.

The next building stage of which evidence will survive (for most of the superstructure has usually disappeared) will be the laying down of the floors. Sometimes these, which may be of any material from beaten earth to hard cement, are laid direct on the pre-existing levels. More often there is a soil make-up, perhaps because this is a convenient way of disposing of the surplus soil from the foundation-trenches. Sometimes this make-up is substantial, particularly when the previous surface was uneven or sloping. The existence of such make-up increases the chance that there will be objects of possibly considerably earlier date beneath the floor, for the material may have come from anywhere, but of course, as described on p. 71, there can be nothing later than the building date. The fact that such material is make-up and does not contain or overlie the floor is usually clear from the absence below or within it of any suitable hard level for the floor, and also from the character of the wall. This will be free-built, but will not have the flush face described above. Occasionally the pre-existing surface may be actually cut away, either in the process of levelling off a site, or to make a sunk chamber such as a cellar or hypocaust. This will usually be clear by reference to the levels in adjoining areas.

The original walls of any one room will clearly be associated with the same floor levels. The junctions of the foundations of the walls may be actually bonded in, thus making their contemporaneity certain. It should however be noted that sometimes when a later wall is put in, part of the face of the original one is cut out and a new patch put in, which bonds in with the new wall; such a false bond can however usually be detected on examination. The lack of bonding in foundations does not, nevertheless, prove that the walls are not contemporary. Foundations of cross walls are often built with butt-joints against the main walls, the two bonding in above ground level. But even if the superstructure does not survive, the relationship can be established by reference to the floor and other levels.

It often happens that additions and alterations are made in the course of the life of a building. The simplest addition is that of a new floor level, which must be identified since it may seal objects later than the original date of the building. It is usually quite simple to do so, since beneath it will be another adequate surface sealing the foundation-trench. Difficulties only arise if the secondary floor replaces one which has been worn away, but there are usually signs of this in some part of the area.

An additional wall will cut the original floor and make-up, and thus its secondary character will be clear. Its structural relationship, either not bonded or with a false bond, will also provide evidence.

It sometimes happens that original walls are partly rebuilt at the time of such alterations; such rebuildings can generally be identified by slight differences in technique, in the bond, the building material and size of stones, while often there is a slight alteration in the colour of the mortar. Stratification will as a rule give the clue, but structural features must also be given full consideration; if the structural evidence is absolutely definite and does not accord with the stratigraphical, it must be given the preponderant weight, and some other explanation of the stratification must be sought. The additions and alterations may be complex, and each must be worked out in a similar way.

In some alterations original walls may be abolished. Their remains will then be sealed by a floor of a subsequent phase (Fig. 2). This removal may be complete, leaving in fact only a robber-trench of the type described on p. 75. The line of the walls will however be visible in section and in the breaks in floor surfaces. In the search for any such vanished walls, it is important to remember that any discrepancies in stratification must be accounted for. For instance, if the floor contemporary with a single north-south wall is on two different levels, there must be a cross wall running east-west in between and this must be found.

Sometimes even in quite substantial structures, subsidiary walls may be of slight character, such as lath and plaster. The only traces of these will be breaks in the floor levels and sometimes the holes in which the more substantial timbers have decayed.

There are in fact many variations in the structural methods employed in buildings of the type found on Roman or Mediaeval sites. The more substantial are built throughout of stone and brick, the stone varying according to the locality. In other cases they may be partly of stone and partly of timber, the foundations usually being of stone, often with sockets for the main timbers. Again, they may be completely of timber. In such cases it is quite usual for the uprights to be set in a horizontal timber or sleeper-beam at the base. The only trace of this which would survive in most soils is a slot of dark soft earth (Pl. 4). This is quite easily traceable, and its position is also often indicated by the edge of the floor. Other timber walls may be of substantial uprights at intervals with slighter posts in between. These can again be traced by discolouration and soft filling in their sockets. A variety of the timber wall is the wattle-and-

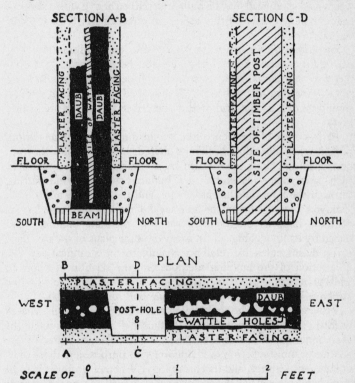

Fig. 4. Section and plan of wattle-and-daub wall. Section A—B is through daub and wattling, C—D through a main timber. (From Archaeologia 90, Excavations at Verulamium Insula XVII, *by Miss K. M. Richardson.)*

daub wall, which is employed both in Roman, prehistoric and Mediaeval structures. This is a wall which usually again has substantial uprights at intervals, while in between is hurdling which serves as a stiffening for the clay core of the wall. In a Roman house the surface of the clay would be covered by wall-plaster. The daub usually only survives recognisably if it has been burnt. Such a wattle-and-daub wall may be built as described above with a sleeper-beam, or may consist of thin stakes set direct in clay (Pls. 5, 6 and Fig. 4).

Such timber-built structures vary greatly, trom substantial affairs with hard concrete floors, to quite slight huts or sheds. It is only the more substantial structures, with well-defined floors, which are suitable for digging by the method described in this section. Others should be dug by the grid method described below for prehistoric sites.

In the course of the occupation of a site during the Roman period, not only are individual buildings altered, but sometimes they are destroyed and their place taken by completely different ones. In such cases, the walls of the new building will be found cutting through the floors of the earlier one, and the latter's walls will be removed at least to below the floor level of the new one (unless some of them happen to be incorporated in the new building) and sealed by its floors (Fig. 2). In excavation the plans of the two have to be disentangled by reference mainly to the stratification. The description of the building methods and the relation of floors to walls given in the preceding paragraphs of course apply equally to a structure succeeding another as to one built on virgin soil.

From considering how a building was constructed we can proceed to methods of excavation. The main aims in dealing with a site of the type under consideration are to establish the plan, or plans if there are one or more superimposed buildings, its purpose and those of its component features, and its chronology. Whether or not it is to be completely cleared will depend on resources available, on the intrinsic importance of the building and whether it is to remain open or to be filled in again.

In such a site, the unit of clearance is best formed by the actual rooms of the structure itself, and not by the artificial units which, as will be seen, are necessary in some other types of site. The first step must therefore be to delimit these rooms, which is done by cutting a series of trenches. These trenches should be at right angles to the walls of the structure. On some sites, the alignment of the structure may be indicated beforehand. For instance, if the site is on the brow of a slope, the probability is that the structure will lie along the brow. If there is a known road line, the structure will probably have a frontage parallel to it. If there is no indication of the line, the first trench must be an exploratory one; once the line of the walls has been established the rest of the trenches should be adjusted to be at right angles to them.

The trenches must be accurately and tidily laid out. They must be lined out with string, as described on p. 77, and their width accurately measured at both ends. The actual width will depend on the depth to which they will have to be dug. Three feet is a minimum width; anything narrower is awkward to work in, and one cannot get far away from the face to see the section properly. If the first trenches show that there is a depth of more than three feet to be dug, subsequent trenches should be wider.

The plan of campaign should be carefully thought out in the initial stages, and will again depend on the type of site and the resources available. If the intention is only to trace the plan and establish the chronology, the earth from the trenches may be dumped along (or rather, at least one foot back from) their edges, provided that the depth is not so great as to produce an unwieldly bulk of spoil. If it is hoped to uncover the whole building, the earth must be dumped clear of the site, and this should be done from the start, as double shifting of spoil is a nuisance. It is in any case advisable to start by delimiting the site, or building within a larger site, by cutting a trench right across it in both directions. This will indicate the type of structure and floors, and the depth of soil, and may suggest which are the principal rooms.

These preliminary trenches should ordinarily be carried down to the highest floor levels only, in the first stage. The next step is to trace the plan. This should be done by a series of trenches at right angles to the first ones. That is to say, between each pair of walls crossing the trench, another trench is run at right angles to delimit the four sides of the room. The process is continued until the whole plan is clear (Fig. 5). It may happen that, as is described above (p. 75), the walls have been robbed out below floor level. Their position will be indicated by a break in the floor level, which will be picked up again after a gap. The process of tracing such robbed

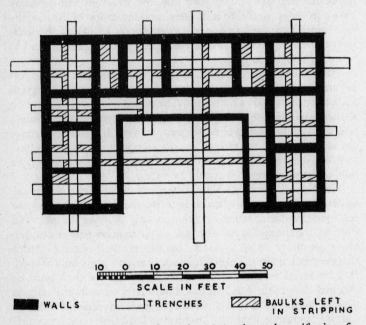

Fig. 5. Diagram to illustrate the tracing of the plan and stratification of a masonry building by trenches, and the baulks which should be left standing until the last stages if the building is being completely cleared.

walls is essentially similar to that of tracing standing walls, by a series of trenches at right angles to their line, which can then be planned by joining up the series of breaks in the floor, though of course with some margin of uncertainty, since the gap may be wider than the robbed wall.

The next step will depend on whether the site or the portion in

question is to be completely cleared or not. If so, it is convenient
to remove the rest of the upper soil at this stage, since it makes
digging lower levels easier and enables the upper level to be photographed as a whole. But it is essential to leave keys or baulks of
upper soil standing, so that eventually a complete section can be
obtained from top to bottom, since often further excavation will raise
new points of interpretation, and one must be able to refer back to a
visible section to decide them. In most cases these sections should
be left crossing each room in both directions (Fig. 5), so that there
are sections against all the walls, but this may be modified in special
circumstances.

After this has been done, or, if clearance is not being undertaken,
with the omission of this stage, the next step is to cut through the
floors, to establish what are the underlying levels. This may be done
by continuing down the original trenches, unless factors revealed in
excavation suggest that other positions will be more useful. If these
trenches show that the site is a simple one, with no underlying
structures, all that has to be done is to ensure that the history of the
whole building is the same, by cutting a sufficient number of
sections, ideally up to all the walls.

If, on the other hand, the site is complicated by a number of
periods, these will have to be worked out. On sites where total
clearance is being carried out, it is convenient, if it is found that there
are lower floors, to remove the upper ones at this stage, always, as
described above, leaving complete sections in each area. If the site is
not being cleared, it is simply a matter of carrying the trenches to the
requisite depth, and making sure that the floor levels in the different
trenches are correctly correlated. It is particularly important to
ascertain whether all walls are contemporary with the original floor,
if there are several floor levels.

On sites where there is a different building below the uppermost,
the process of tracing is a repetition of that of tracing the upper
one. It is convenient to finish dealing with the upper one first. If
the area is to be cleared, all its layers can then be stripped off. This
must be done in strict chronological order. The first step is to
remove all disturbances, for instance the fill of the robber trenches

from which walls have been removed and of any pits cutting into the structure, for these are clearly subsequent to the use of the house. Then would follow any occupation on the floors, any additional floors, and finally the original floors, their make-up, and the contents of the foundation-trenches. If any of this fill is accidentally left behind, its contents may confuse the evidence with reference to the lower structures. It may be desirable to remove some of its walls if it obscures features of the lower building, but this should not be done unnecessarily. It is probable that some at least of the baulks left standing across the rooms of the upper building may have to be removed, to enable the lower one to be cleared, but enough should be retained to enable the stratification of the lower building to be connected with that of the upper one. If the site is not being completely cleared, the trenching process is continued until the plan of the lower building is completed. It may at this stage be necessary to dig new trenches from the surface to trace walls or examine points which do not occur in trenches planned to deal with the upper structure. If the succession is complicated and there are several structures one above the other, and particularly if there is any great depth of deposit, it becomes essential to clear away the surface soil and deposits belonging to the upper building completely, as it is both uneconomic and unsatisfactory to examine things at the bottom of deep trenches. Six feet is the maximum depth of deposit for which it is suitable to use trenches and this should be exceptional; four feet is about the comfortable limit.

This description of how to excavate a building will have shown how fundamental it is to have sections running up to all the walls, for it is by them that the relationship of the walls to the deposits and their dating material is established. It follows that it is a cardinal error to dig along the line of a wall. Such a trench cuts through the connection of wall and floors or other deposits and destroys the evidence. Before the principles of stratification were understood, the lines of walls were traced by a trench along them, but this nowadays should *never* be done. If a preliminary trench turns out to be alongside or over a wall, it should be suspended as soon as this is realised.

Finally an excavation should not be begun unless it is intended to finish it, for subsequent excavators are not readily attracted by a partially excavated site, and information about it will be apt to remain permanently inadequate. The completeness should be both horizontal and vertical. That is to say, in the first place the plan should be complete. It should be remembered that Roman villas, for instance, are complex affairs like modern farm buildings. The dwelling-house nearly always has adjuncts in the way of barns, labourers' quarters and so on, and the picture is far more valuable if it provides information about such buildings. Therefore, if the area adjoining a site on which a villa has been identified is available, it should be trenched in an endeavour to locate these adjuncts. This doctrine does not of course mean that one must excavate a whole Roman town if one starts on any part of it. The buildings within it can be treated as entities, though of course a far greater contribution to knowledge can be made if at least an *insula* can be excavated. To the second necessity, complete vertical excavation, there should be no exception. All areas should be at least tested to virgin soil. If they are not, an unexpected earlier occupation may not be discovered, and will probably be permanently lost, for future excavators will not wish to remove earth disturbed by predecessors on the chance of finding something below. It may happen that there is some structure, such as a mosaic floor, which it is not wished to destroy, but in that case adjacent areas can usually be tested to reduce to a minimum the chance of anything important being overlooked.

Excavation of a Prehistoric Occupation Site. There are two main reasons why a prehistoric site requires a slightly different method of excavation from that described in the last section. The first is that its remains, other than the surrounding earthworks, the excavation of which is described in the next section, are much slighter than those of a masonry-built structure. The floors are usually of trodden earth, and the walls of perishable materials such as timber or turf. Such remains are not easy to spot in the comparatively limited space of the floor of a trench, and one requires a larger horizontal area in order to recognise their significance. The second reason is that the plan of prehistoric structures is much more irregular. One cannot, having found a wall in one trench, predict that one will pick up its continuation in a straight line in the next one. Also the various adjuncts of a prehistoric dwelling are complicated and irregularly arranged. Therefore, the only safe way to dig a prehistoric site is to clear a fairly large horizontal area.

Again, before the method of excavating such a site is described, it is necessary to understand of what it may consist and how the buildings are constructed. The unit of the most usual type of pre-historic site found in southern Britain is a hut, which can be of very varying size. This may be surrounded by a number of accessory structures. The most important are varieties of storage pits, for corn, water and so on. As discovered, these are simply pits of varying dimensions and shapes, but they may originally have been lined by some material such as skin, which has perished. Often there is also a bewildering mass of post-holes in the surrounding area. These have been identified as traces of the supports of various other storage containers and also other structures connected with agricultural operations. For instance, it is suggested that groups of four posts close together supported bins for storing seed corn. This could not be parched, as had to be done with that stored in pits to prevent it getting mouldy, so it had to be stored above ground, away from damp and animals. Pairs or lines of post-holes may have held the uprights or racks for drying hay, while single posts may have been the centre support of haystacks of the small conical type found in some continental countries today. Other remains may include the bases of clay ovens in which the corn was roasted. In a number of instances irregular hollows have been found which were apparently working floors where the corn was thrashed. Drainage channels to assist in the collection of water are often found. Finally, there may be traces of the fences of pens in which stock could be herded.

The huts themselves can vary greatly from a quite modest size to others which were 100 feet across. They are usually round, but may be rectangular. The latter usually have a central ridge pole with an upright support at either end, with the roof sloping down on either side to lower side walls, while the normal round huts have a central pole, or sometimes a structure of four poles from which the roof sloped down to a single or double ring of outer posts. The roofs were probably thatched, while the walls might be of daub, timber or brushwood. Other huts may have at least the base of the walls made of turf.

All these structures had a comparatively short existence. As modern experience shows, wooden posts set in the ground rot away below ground level and have to be replaced. Therefore the posts of both the huts and subsidiary structures usually show signs of renewal if the settlement has been in occupation any length of time. The storage pits would tend to be fouled by vermin and fungi, and would in due course be abandoned. It is of their use at this stage that we usually find evidence, for they are nearly always found filled with occupation rubbish. Primitive people do not as a rule dig pits on purpose to dispose of rubbish, but when a pit ceased to be used for its original function, it was convenient to fill it by dumping in it any rubbish lying about. Sometimes this filling shows stages. Hearths may be found in such pits suggesting that they were used for cooking in rough weather. Occasionally the family may have sheltered in them, particularly on an exposed site like Maiden Castle, where evidence was found in one pit that a group squatted on the floor and threw the bones of their meal over their shoulders. But such use is exceptional. The old view that these pits represented dwellings is now recognised as erroneous. The primary purpose was storage; other uses were subsidiary.

Such huts and their accessory structures may be isolated, and represent scattered farmsteads. The farmstead may be open, with just a fence around it, or it may, for at least part of its lifetime, have been protected by an encircling earthwork. Alternatively, they may be grouped in villages or even towns, of which last the best known example is Maiden Castle in Dorset. The component features will vary, the accessory structures of an isolated farmstead such as Little Woodbury, Wiltshire, being more complex and widespread than in the more congested area of Maiden Castle, but they are basically similar, and require the same excavation technique.

In all cases it must be remembered that it is probable that at no time were all the huts, pits and structures represented by post-holes in use at one time. Sometimes stratification will enable a sequence to be established, but this is not so precise a guide as on, for instance, a Roman site. Floor levels are much slighter, and are apt to be worn away by use, while the area surrounding the structures as a rule had no made surface, wear tending in fact to work down into pre-existing levels. The succession therefore has to be worked out mainly from inferences from juxtaposition, and from contents of pits if this is diagnostic, aided by such items of stratification as survive.

While the type of prehistoric occupation just described is now well-known in southern Britain, other types exist elsewhere, and it is by no means certain that we yet know all varieties. For instance, at Sutton Walls in Herefordshire, excavation has recently shown that occupation is concentrated in a series of fairly widely spaced scoops or hollows up to 70 feet in diameter, while accessory storage pits and probably other structures seem to be lacking. In the highland zones of England, Wales and Scotland, huts were mainly constructed of the readily available local stone, usually with very slight foundations, and sometimes combined with timber posts for stability. Sometimes, as at Skara Brae in the Orkneys, these stone structures are very complex, while in other cases all that survive are simple rings of stones forming the bases of the huts. On these types of sites, there is so far little evidence of associated pits and other structures, perhaps because the land was not suitable for agriculture, and the economy was primarily pastoral.

But all these types of occupation share the characteristics that the plan is irregular and the remains comparatively slight. They therefore all require to be excavated by a method which completely exposes a substantial horizontal area, so that the various irregularly situated components can all be identified, and so that features such as the edge of a slight earth floor can be seen as a whole, and thus identified.

The method of excavation is therefore to combine the complete clearance of a selected area with the recording of stratification. One method is to clear a succession of strips across the site, the spoil from each strip being filled back into the last completed one. This has the advantage that the labour of shifting soil is reduced, but the disadvantages that no transverse sections across the site are preserved, while a large structure, such as a hut, which may stretch across more than one strip, is never completely visible at one time, though such visual evidence is often very helpful to interpretation.

The most satisfactory method is undoubtedly the grid system, in which the site is excavated in a series of squares, separated by baulks which are left standing and which thus provide keys to the stratification (Pl. 8). The size of the squares and width of the baulks will depend on the depth of the excavation and the type of soil. For most sites in this country a square with a side of 10 or 12 feet will be the most convenient, divided from the next by a baulk 2 feet wide, though if the soil is unstable or the depth very great 3 feet may be advisable.

The first step will be to lay out the grid accurately over the initial area of excavation (it can be subsequently extended). Care must be taken to line through the squares accurately and to ensure that they are truly right-angled. The exact corners of the squares should be marked with pegs and string stretched between to mark out the edges, but these pegs cannot remain in position as the square is excavated, for they will be dislodged by the removal of earth. Therefore the permanent record pegs must be set back in the centre of the baulk. These should be of 2 ins × 2 ins timber, and should be set diagonally, so that on the face towards each adjacent square the number of the square can be painted. In the top a nail should be driven, from which measurements can be taken.

Since the area selected is to be totally excavated, the spoil-earth must be dumped clear. On a site about which nothing is known, it may be necessary to put down some trial trenches first in order to find whether the occupation is continuous, or, if it is not, where it is concentrated. These trenches should be planned so that any of them can be developed into squares if required, that is to say, transverse baulks at the distances and of the width decided upon for the squares should be left across the trenches. In this preliminary stage, the spoil may be dumped beside the trenches, but as soon as it has been decided which area is to be opened up, the spoil should be transferred to an area outside that planned for the season's excavations.

Each square is treated as the unit of excavation. The first step is most conveniently to remove the humus or plough soil all over the square, which can be done by unskilled navvy labour, if such is being employed. When clearance of this has been completed, a trench should be sunk along one side of the square until the first apparent surface is reached. The rest of the square should then be cleared in any layers which the first trench has revealed, down to this surface. If this surface appears to be a definite floor, and extends into adjoining squares, these should be cleared in a similar manner to the same depth, so that the whole of the structure may be visible at the same time, which renders the interpretation much easier. The keys formed by the baulks of the squares should however be left standing, unless there is a strong reason for the contrary, such as the need for an unobstructed photograph of an important structure. If they are to be removed, their stratification must of course be drawn first, as is described in the section on Records, and when excavation is continued downwards, the lower part of the fill must be left as a baulk in the same position.

The slightness of the structural evidence on many prehistoric sites has been emphasized in the preceding paragraphs. Therefore it is necessary that great care should be taken to observe all traces. The surfaces of all layers must be carefully scraped and brushed, so that any lines or patches of discolouration may show up. Post-holes will be indicated by patches, usually of soft dark earth. The identification of such post-holes requires some experience, for if an inexperienced worker starts digging out patches which he imagines to be post-holes, it is very difficult to check afterwards whether he is right or not. The edges of post-holes will be usually quite well-defined, and will 'make themselves' if the filling in the centre is carefully cleared out. The shape will usually be approximately circular, if untrimmed timbers have been used, while trimmed timber will probably be rectangular. Both will probably taper to the base if they have been driven into soft soil, while if a pit has had to be cut for them in

10. *Planning with tapes and plumb-bob from two fixed points.*

11. Measuring a section with horizontal string, tape and five-foot rod.

solid soil, such as chalk, the posts will have been wedged by stones, which often survive in position after the timber has decayed away.

The edges of huts will often best be defined by the edge of the floor. Even if this is no more than the trodden surface of the underlying soil, the hardening will cease on the line of the wall of the hut. The traces of the actual wall will depend on its material. There will usually be some posts, though sometimes the roof may slope down from a central post or ridge on to a wall of turf or possibly a dry-stone wall. Turf will of course have decayed, but it usually shows up as a greyish or blackish band against the surrounding soil. If cut through, the layering of the actual turves may be visible. A wall of wattle-and-daub will only have retained its shape if it was burnt, as sometimes happens in the destruction of the hut. A rather amorphous band of clay may however survive to indicate the base of the wall. Dry-stone walling requires no special description.

Pits will define themselves by patches of soft soil or by upper strata dipping into them, due to the gradual sinkage of unconsolidated material. The method of excavation of pits will depend on their size. The layers in them must be recorded, for they provide evidence as to whether the fill is homogeneous or has various periods in it. The ideal method is to excavate half the filling, layer by layer, leaving the other half standing, so as to provide a section which can be drawn. If the pit is too small for this to be physically possible, it will have to be done stage by stage, one half being excavated for, say, 1 foot, the section drawn with reference to some well-defined datum point (Chapter VI), then the second half removed, and the process repeated until the bottom of the pit is reached. It is very important that it should be clear from which level a pit is dug. This is one of the reasons why all surfaces should be carefully swept as work proceeds, so that the first appearance of the pit can be spotted. It should then be related to one of the standing keys by tracing the relevant layers to it, so that its place in the sequence can be understood.

Once all the components—structures, pits, post-holes—of the uppermost level have been identified, excavated, planned and photographed, the excavation should be continued down, first by a trench, and then, if earlier levels are found beneath, by further clearance, and the process repeated.

If there are structures one above the other, or cutting into each other, stratification will provide the key to the succession. If they do not overlie or cut into each other, and the associated surfaces in fact represent a gradual wearing away of pre-existing levels, as is often the case, the succession or contemporaneity may be a matter of inference. If the pottery or other material shows a development, or new influences, the contents of hut floors or the occupation upon them, or of the fill of pits, will help to establish this succession. Otherwise it may be a matter or probabilities, but usually there are some points which make it possible to decide the question of whether or not occupation has covered a prolonged period.

The Excavation of Tells.   *Tell* is a term used in Arabic-speaking countries for an artificial mound which has been formed by human occupation over a long period. In Turkish the word used is *hüyük*, in Persian *tepe*, but the word tell is here used as a generic term, for the problems in all these Eastern countries are the same. It is of course obvious that no beginner should be allowed to be responsible for the excavation of such a site. But sometimes comparative beginners go out to assist on such sites, and therefore a description of the correct method of excavation is here included so that such a beginner may start with some knowledge of the problems involved.

The reason that tells are more common in Eastern countries than in Europe is mainly that settled urban life has existed in them for millennia, whereas in most of Europe it has existed only for a matter of centuries. One village or town has been built on top of the ruins of its predecessor often continuously from Neolithic times even to modern days, or at any rate for a considerable part of that period. As buildings in each town became ruinous or were destroyed, their remains were levelled over and others built on top of them. In this way the ground level of the settlement was gradually raised, so that while the earliest occupation may have been on the level of a surrounding plain, the latest may be on a mound rising sixty or a hundred feet above it. The instances given of length of occupation

THE TECHNIQUE OF FIELD WORK: EXCAVATING   99

and depth of deposit may be extreme ones, and many sites have had
a much shorter life and much smaller depth of deposit, but a great
number of such sites do present to excavators the problem of dealing
with a complicated series of superimposed occupation levels.

This problem of superimposed levels is common to all such sites.
There are, however, two different types of sites within the main
group which have separate problems, the sites where the buildings
are of mud-brick and those where they are of stone. The methods
of excavation are basically the same, but the differences in the
development of the sites require some description.

The interpretation of a site of mud-brick buildings is of the two
the simpler, though the technique of tracing the buildings is more
difficult. The reason that the interpretation of a mud-brick site is the
simpler is twofold. Mud-brick, once it is in position, cannot be
re-used, and therefore subsequent builders do not dig down into the
houses of their predecessors in order to obtain building materials.
Secondly, a mud-brick building when destroyed or decayed creates
out of itself, from the decay of its mud-bricks, a great depth of soil,
and thus forms a thick layer over the remains of one building stage,
on top of which the next is built. The different phases therefore tend
to be well marked and well separated from each other. It does not
follow that the same phases are present all over the tell, and at the
same level, as the earlier excavators, working after Flinders Petrie
had enunciated this general principle of basic stratigraphy in 1890,
tended to expect. One section of a town might be destroyed and
rebuilt while another remained standing; an important building like
a temple might be retained unmodified while other areas were
renewed; in a less prosperous period, only the centre of the town
might be occupied while the rest was in ruins, and it would therefore
grow in height while the outskirts did not. It is therefore clear that
relating together different parts of the tell by absolute heights above
sea-level is in any case meaningless, and such evidence is made more
so by the fact that it takes no account of disturbances such as
foundation-trenches, pits and so on. It is therefore no less important to ascribe objects to the correct phase by the exact strata of the
soil in this type than in any other type of excavation.

The great difficulty in excavating a mud-brick site as opposed to one built in stone lies in the need for considerable skill in tracing the walls. The mud-brick is usually the colour of the surrounding soil, for it is made out of it. Moreover, within the area of the rooms will be great masses of mud-brick fallen from the upper part of the building, tending to form an almost solid mass with the standing walls. The technique of tracing the actual walls is largely a matter of practice, in which the native workman often becomes highly skilled. Consistency, feel, and the sound of the pick or other tool all enter into it. The courses of the standing wall can with care be made visible and are obviously regular and horizontal, while those in a fallen mass are unlikely to be. But all these points must be learnt by practice under trained guidance.

The special difficulties of a stone-built eastern site are fourfold. In the first place, such sites are usually in hill country, for it is there that building stone is available. The settlements are therefore usually on hill-tops, and so start from an uneven basis, which makes the correlation of the different areas more difficult. Secondly, the destruction of a building does not produce the depth of deposit that a mud-brick building does. The stones from the collapsed or destroyed superstructure will almost certainly be re-used by the next builders. The levels of the successive phases are therefore much closer together and less well-defined. Thirdly, it was often easier to obtain further building stone from the remains of earlier structures than to quarry it afresh, so that in addition to using stones from collapsed walls, subsequent builders often dug out early walls to a great depth. The sites are therefore apt to be seamed with robber-trenches. Finally, the foundations of stone buildings are usually deeper than those of mud-brick, and walls of the more important buildings are often carried down to rock, or to some solid earlier structure. Earlier levels are therefore liable to be extensively cut by later walls, leading to a maze of foundations of different periods side by side. A typical section from the excavations at Samaria in Palestine is illustrated in Fig. 6. All these difficulties are similar to those one may find on sites of masonry structures in Britain, but intensified by the greater length of occupation and depth of deposit.

SECTION E - F

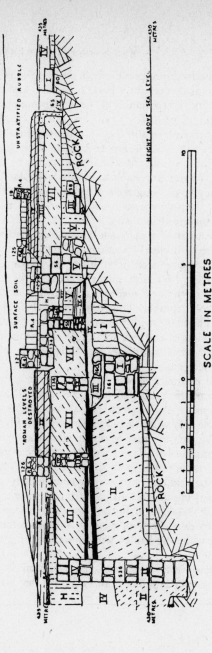

UNSTRATIFIED RUBBLE

SURFACE SOIL

ROMAN LEVELS DESTROYED

ROCK

ROCK

HEIGHT ABOVE SEA LEVEL

SCALE IN METRES

Fig. 6. Section through the northern side of the summit of the town of Samaria, Palestine, to illustrate the complex succession of levels and walls on an Eastern site. Periods I–VI are Israelite, 9th to 8th centuries, VII represents the Assyrian destruction in 720 B.C., and the overlying levels cover the 7th century B.C. to the 4th century A.D. Note the deep robbing of earlier walls. (From Samaria–Sebaste I, by Crowfoot, Kenyon and Sukenik.)

The basic method of interpretation of both types of tell sites should be the same as that employed on occupation sites in Britain. It is dependent on the interpretation of the stratification in the same exact way, so that it is possible to establish the relationship of all the walls to the adjacent layers in the soil. Therefore no more on a tell than in Britain should clearance be carried down all over the area at the same time, as it all too often is. Even on an apparently simple site, such as a great Assyrian palace with walls standing many feet high, there may be pits dug right down through the filling of a room, introducing late objects at floor level. Key sections are as necessary here as on any British site.

In order to obtain at all a complete knowledge of the different phases of a tell site, it is clearly necessary to remove each level in turn over a considerable area. The lower levels can never be adequately explored by trenching, since not enough will be exposed. It is true that the method of *sondage* is sometimes employed, in which a shaft of comparatively limited area is sunk to the bottom of the tell. This is however with the avowed object of establishing what is the succession of cultures and range of occupation on the site, and is justified for this purpose, but it gives little information as to the type of occupation.

The method of clearance should therefore be an adaptation of the grid system employed on British prehistoric sites. It is necessary to adopt an arbitrary unit like this, because superimposed on one another in the same area will probably be a number of buildings of varying orientation, and in order to obtain stratification keys from the top to the bottom of the layers one can only use an arbitrary layout, for no orientation will fit all successive buildings. The size of the squares of the grid must however be considerably larger than on British sites, owing to the probably much greater depth of deposit. The length should probably be something in the neighbourhood of twenty to thirty feet, or at least as long as the expected depth of deposit, while the baulks will have to be proportionately broader.

Within the squares, excavation should be carried on in the manner described for a masonry building in this country, that is to say, the line of the walls of the uppermost layer established, trenches cut at right angles to them (whatever their angle to that of the main grid) and the various layers associated with them identified (Fig. 7). These layers must be correlated with those appearing in the permanent keys provided by the baulks of the squares, so that it is quite clearly recorded, as excavation proceeds lower, which layers in these keys belong to which structural phases.

On a tell dig, it is usually essential to remove each structure, walls and all, after it has been studied and recorded, since otherwise it will be impossible to clear the lower stages. Exceptions sometimes have to be made in favour of exceptionally fine buildings which it would be wrong to destroy, and in these cases the underlying levels have to be sacrificed. The process of removal is similar to that described on p. 90, in connection with British sites; first disturbances such as robber-trenches and pits, then occupation levels, successive floors and their make-ups, foundation-trenches, and finally walls. Owing to conditions governing mud-brick sites, described on p. 99, such removal in their case presents no particular difficulty, once the walls have been traced. The clearance of stone buildings does, however, require further consideration.

The difficulties arise from the close superimposition of the buildings of different periods. The result is that walls of one period often cut deeply into deposits belonging to early ones, and also, if the wall has been dug out, the robber-trenches may cut equally deeply. Ideally, both the walls and the robber-trenches of walls of each period should be removed when work on that period is completed. In practice this may be very difficult. A wall 3 feet wide may have foundations going down 6 or 8 feet. It would be difficult in any case to work in a narrow trench to that depth. It is moreover very difficult to break up a wall working from above, while comparatively simple when working against its face. On the other hand, clearance of earlier levels cannot be continued down flush with its face, for objects from its foundation-trench would contaminate these earlier levels, and still more objects from a robber-trench, to which the same considerations apply. It is therefore necessary first to identify the width of the foundation-trench, or of the robber-trench, by a

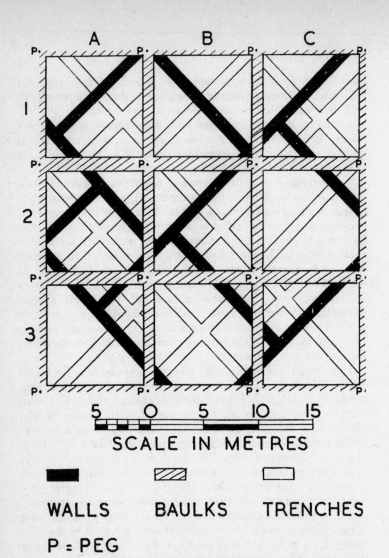

Fig. 7. Diagram to illustrate the excavation of a tell site. The grid of baulks provides the framework for linking the stratification of successive buildings, while within it the lines of, and strata associated with, individual buildings, which may be oblique to the squares, are traced by trenches at right angles to the particular building.

cutting at right angles to it. Then as excavation of the earlier levels into which it cuts continues down, a thin skin of these earlier levels must be left against the intrusive foundation-trench or robber-trench, until its base, as revealed in the exploratory cut, has been reached. Then the fill of the robber-trench or foundation-trench can be removed, together with the skin of earlier levels left against it.

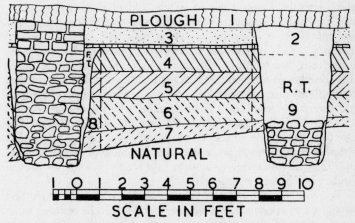

Fig. 8. Diagram to illustrate method of excavating foundations or robber-trenches which are too deep to be removed before the earlier layers through which they cut. The vertical dotted lines indicate the edge of the skin which should be left against them; the numbers show the order in which the different fills should be removed.

(Fig. 8). This will of course mean that objects from this skin belonging to the earlier levels will be included with the later fill, but as described on p. 76, this is much less serious than *vice versa*.

The process of removal layer by layer as just described is then continued right to bed-rock. The policy of how this is done will be affected by the general policy for the whole excavation. It may be the intention to excavate the whole tell completely, though resources very seldom allow of this. For many reasons it may be urged that it is undesirable to attempt this except in the case of small tells. In the first place, to do so depends on being assured of very large funds for an almost unlimited period, and as the history of excavations for the last thirty years in Palestine, for instance, shows, even the richest organizations cannot count on this. Secondly, it means that for many years the excavations will only produce information about the latest, often comparatively uninteresting, periods. Thirdly, the complete excavation of whole phases of major sites means that no part of these phases is left to be checked in the light of future developments. The science of excavation is steadily being improved and modified, as it should be, and it may well be that however carefully the excavations are carried out by present-day standards, future technique would enable still more information to be obtained. The ideal is a compromise, the excavation of a sufficiently large area to enable the plan and type of economy to be adequately investigated, but sufficiently small for it to be possible, with the resources available, to reach the lowest levels all over the area excavated. The complete excavation of a small tell is not ruled out by this, and is valuable in many ways, while such sites are unlikely to be so important that their complete removal would matter, for the results can usually be checked in other sites.

Whether or not a tell is to be completely excavated, the method of approach will depend on whether it has got to be restored to its previous condition or not. If it has not, which is the ideal arrangement from the point of view of the archaeologist, any owners or cultivators will have to be compensated, and the excavator will be free to plan the work as suits him best. In the first place, he will be able to dispose of his spoil so that it does not interfere with his work. It is important, however, to test any dump area, for instance at the foot of the tell, to avoid dumping upon ancient remains, such as tombs. In the second place, he will be able conveniently to excavate all over the area selected, whether the whole tell or a section of it, at the same time, and thus expose the whole of any one phase simultaneously, which is much the best method.

If, however, the ground has got to be restored to its cultivators, the spoil must be kept economically near at hand, for replacement. It would still be possible to excavate the whole area at once, forming a dump which will subsequently have to be filled back. This is, however, an expensive business. The most economical way is for the area selected to be excavated in sections, the spoil from the first section being placed in a dump, that from the second being filled back into the first, the third into the second, and finally the dump into the last. Thus only the spoil from the first section has to be shifted twice.

There are various matters of detail in which the excavation of a tell differs from that of a British site. In the first place, the local labourers may not be used to working with picks and shovels of British type, and it is best to let them use the tools they are accustomed to. In the second, in most eastern sites the practice is to remove soil in baskets instead of throwing it to the surface and then removing it in barrows. This has many advantages, particularly when working at a considerable depth, but involves leaving stair-cases against the side of the cutting, or providing ladders. The greatest difference is the number of workers employed, which is mostly a matter of finance and the availability of labour. But it is most important that each area should be under the supervision of a trained archaeologist or experienced student, and the size of the gangs under a supervisor should not be so great that he cannot keep his eye on all that is going on. Only in this way can the layers be properly observed and the finds recorded, and it is in this respect that so many digs in the east have failed to reach a high standard.

Excavating Earthworks.   Under this heading is included any form of substantial mound or ditch; the two in fact almost invariably go together, for a ditch is the easiest way to obtain material for the bank. Sometimes, however, material for a bank is obtained by surface scrapings or quarryings, and sometimes a bank which has originally existed has been removed, or a ditch has become filled, but is recoverable by excavation. The bank may have associated with it various forms of walling, revetting, or internal structures. The earthworks may surround settlements, or serve as internal divisions in them, or they may be what are known as running earthworks, forming boundaries running across open country.

Earthworks in varying forms are common in all phases of European prehistory and history, from the Neolithic to the Mediaeval periods. In the East, free-standing masonry walls were the traditional method in most cultures. If, however, earthworks of any form are found, the same method of excavation is applicable.

The formation of layers in a bank is of course different from that on an occupation site. They are formed by a series of tips, highest at the crest and tailing down to front and rear. The lines of the tips are mainly caused by variations in material. The bank will probably rest on the pre-existing surface, which may be occupation material or may be natural turf. Occasionally this is stripped off. If the bank was formed from material obtained from cutting a ditch, the first tip, which will form the core of the bank, would be from the surface soil and would include any occupation material lying there, turf and humus; and the rest of the bank will then consist of the various layers of geological material through which the ditch cuts. The ditch cutting may also be supplemented by material from surface scrapings or internal quarrying, or these may even be substituted for it. It is important that the source of the various tips should be identified, so that the evidence from any objects in the bank can be correctly interpreted. In some cases there may be pauses in the construction of a portion of the bank, possibly while other sections are being built, and a hardened surface may be formed. In other instances, additional layers are added at later periods; their identification is discussed below.

Sometimes, as a first step, the line of the bank may be laid out by a slight hollow, such as a plough furrow, or by a low bank, which is subsequently overlaid by the bank, but can be identified in excavation. In construction, the tail of the bank may be allowed to spread, or may be limited by a curb of stones, turf, or a low mound. As regards the front, there are two main types of bank, the type with revetted, vertical face, and the mound type. Of the revetted type, the clearest example is that of the Romano-British town walls, with a solid masonry wall (in front of the bank), which is found in the middle period of the Roman occupation. In the prehistoric period, the revetment may be of drystone walling, of timber, or a combination of the two. The revetment is always associated with a berm, a space between the foot of the revetment and the lip of the ditch, as otherwise the foundations of the revetment would be weakened by the ditch and would tend to slip forward into it. If the revetment is contemporary with the first phase of the bank, it is obviously built first, and the bank piled against its back.

In the mound type of bank, the front and back slope down from the crest at the natural angle of the rest of the soil. The front, like the back, may have a slight curb, or may slope directly down to the lip of the ditch. In such banks, there are sometimes traces of a palisade, of timber or stone, on the crest. It is in fact probable that such a palisade existed in most cases, since a sloping mound is not a very complete obstacle, but often the crest is too denuded for traces to survive.

The core of the bank may be strengthened by internal walls. These may be parallel to the line of the bank, or may be more elaborate, forming a series of cells. It is usually clear from their appearance that they were always meant to be buried, and that their purpose was only to prevent the core slipping.

Objects beneath and in the bank will provide at least a *terminus post quem* for its construction. If there is an actual occupation level beneath the bank, it may represent the stage immediately prior to the turf construction. If they are in a turf level, which can usually be recognised by its greyish colour and rather sticky texture, they may belong to a considerably earlier period. The significance of objects in the core of the bank depends to some extent on the material they are in. If they are in what looks like surface scrapings, they probably represent earlier occupation levels. If they are in the material from the top of the ditch, forming the lowest level of the bank, they may have been on the surface or in the turf at the time. If they are in the material from lower in the ditch, cut into the natural subsoil, they have probably been dropped by the actual builders of the bank. There is of course a chance that the builders may have dropped objects into any of the layers of the bank, but one cannot count on this. Safer evidence concerning the builders is provided by traces of immediately succeeding occupation, for instance in a quarry scoop at the rear, or overlaid by the primary spread from the bank.

Good evidence about the builders is also often provided by the ditch. After the ditch has been cut, there is usually some weathering of the sides, forming a deposit known as rapid silt. Objects in this often belong to the first occupants of the site after the ditch has been cut, though earlier objects may be included. Above this will be found material from the bank after it has started to decay, which may include objects from the bank and also those belonging to subsequent occupations of the site.

Banks often show more than one period of construction. This is best shown by traces of a turf line covering the original bank and sealed by the later layers. Often it is associated with different structural features, such as a renewal of the revetment, or a change to the mound type of bank after the revetment has collapsed. The ditch may be re-cut at the same time. This is sometimes difficult to detect, unless portions of the earlier silt have been left in position.

Earthworks which are not associated with occupation sites are often more difficult to date, for there is not much probability that they will contain objects. The best chance of obtaining an indication of their date is to excavate them in the neighbourhood of some occupation site, where the presence or absence of objects of the period of that settlement will provide at least a *terminus post* or *ante quem* for the construction.

The method of excavating all earthworks is to make a cutting through them at right angles, so as to establish the layers in them (Pl. 9). The width of the cutting will depend on the depth. A width of 6 feet is a minimum for all but the most insignificant banks or ditches, and it will often need to be much more. The depth of cuttings both through banks and ditches is often such that a vertical side to the trench will not stand. The alternatives in this case are to dig the sides on a batter converging gently towards the bottom, or to timber the sides as digging proceeds. Both are tiresome procedures, the latter more so, since it means that the layers can never be seen as a whole. Advice on the method to use should be obtained from someone who knows the local soil. Timbering also requires skilled advice.

The disposal of soil in a dig through an earthwork is usually rather difficult. In the first place, as soon as the trench becomes deep, double-chucking will be necessary, and a series of steps must be left to form platforms for this. Secondly the spoil, when thrown on to the side, will tend to slip to the bottom of the bank or ditch, which if allowed would increase greatly the labour of refilling, and it is necessary to build a series of revetting walls to hold it up. Thirdly, it must be kept well back from the sides of the trench, as otherwise its weight will increase the chance of the sides of the trench collapsing.

Evidence for the date of the bank is provided by the objects in it, and, as has been described, it is important to know in what layer they were. Digging is carried out as far as possible by layers, but if these are, as they may be, on a steep slope, it is sometimes difficult to be absolutely certain in which layer an object is, for the bulk of earth to be shifted makes it impracticable to excavate an earthwork by trowel. It is therefore necessary to employ the three-dimensional method of recording described on pp. 133-4.

The Excavation of Burials.   Ancient burials may be of a number of different types. They may be in long or round tumuli or cairns, they may be in chamber tombs or they may be simple graves containing single burials, which may again be inhumations or cremations.

It is now recognised that the excavation of a round barrow or tumulus is a much more complicated procedure than was considered necessary in the old days, when a trench was simply cut through the middle. This is because such tumuli usually include elaborate structures, such as timber circles, stone settings, trodden areas, turf mounds and so on, from which various elements connected with the ritual of the burial have been deduced. It is therefore necessary to excavate the whole area to ensure that nothing is missed. Moreover, there are very often secondary burials, sometimes of a considerably later period, inserted in various parts of the mound, while the primary burial, usually a cremation if the tumulus belongs to the Bronze Age, is in the centre.

Before excavation begins, a contour plan must be made of the whole mound. This is necessary as a record, since the mound will be destroyed in excavation, and may also give an indication of features not apparent to the eye.

One method employed for such total excavation is to work through the mound from one end to another in a series of slices. This will give a succession of sections across the mound on one axis, but has the disadvantage that it gives none in the opposite direction. A more satisfactory way is to excavate it by segments (Pl. 7), leaving a key in each direction. The segments should be staggered, so that one face of the key only is continuous across the whole mound. This avoids the risk of some feature in the centre being completely beneath the key (Fig. 9).

Within the segments, the position of all objects and burials found should be correctly recorded by the three-dimensional method (pp. 133-4). The significance of all the structural features or surfaces must be carefully worked out, and even those which seem incomprehensible should be accurately planned. No one should attempt to excavate a tumulus without first reading reports of recent excavations and the material they have produced.

A long barrow is again a complex structure and also requires complete excavation. The method is similar, except that the length requires a number of cross-sections to be left in addition to a longitudinal one, and it should in fact be excavated in a number of bays. The structural features are usually elaborate, and the position of all stones may have to be planned in the case of badly destroyed mounds, in order to recover as much evidence as possible. In the great majority of cases, the primary burials in the central chamber have been disturbed.

Chamber tombs are the type most commonly found in the East. They may be in natural caves or artificially excavated chambers. The great majority contain multiple burials. Ideally they should be excavated by sectors, so that a section in each direction can be drawn, but sometimes the size makes this difficult. In point of fact, they seldom provide evidence of a series of undisturbed layers of burials, since in many instances on each occasion that a new burial was inserted the bones and offerings belonging to previous ones were pushed towards the back. It is therefore often very difficult to establish which objects were associated with which burial, though

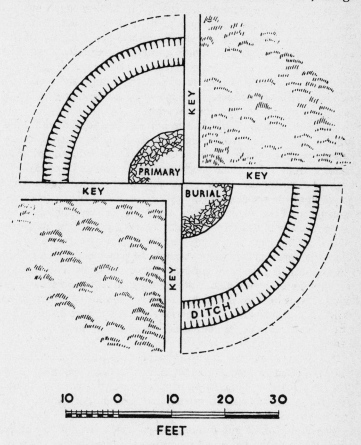

Fig. 9. Method of excavating a round barrow by quadrants, the junction of the quadrants being staggered to ensure that important deposits in the centre should not be left covered by the keys. Two opposite quadrants should be first cleared, followed by the remaining pair, the keys being left standing.

any evidence for this should be carefully recorded, and also any evidence bearing on succession. The position of each object should be exactly recorded on the plan, as that should of all skeletal remains, to enable all possible deductions to be made from association or position, and if there are any significant layers, the relation of the objects and burial to them should of course be recorded. As on a tell, the absolute level of the objects is unlikely to have much significance, unless it is clear from the stratification and condition of the burials that interments were in fact placed one above the other without the earlier ones being disturbed.

In the excavation of inhumation burials, stratification within the grave is unlikely to have any significance, though it must of course be ascertained from what level the grave was dug. This can probably be done from the first cut which reveals the grave. Once this has been established, the whole grave should be cleared down from above until the skeleton is reached. It is inadvisable to clean the skeleton until the whole of the upper filling has been removed, as otherwise it is almost impossible to prevent earth falling on to the cleared portion, and also to prevent damage to the exposed bones. Once the upper fill has been removed, the skeleton should be carefully cleaned and the earth cut away round the edges of the bones. The individual bones should not be lifted in this process, as it is difficult to restore them firmly to their positions. A knife, paint brush, and, if the soil is dry, bellows, are the most useful tools for this. When this has been completed, the skeleton should be photographed and planned.

The excavation of cremation burials raises no particular problems. They are usually found in containers, such as urns, and it is simply a matter of clearing the urns, and any accessory objects, as carefully as possible. Such burials are often found in groups, or urnfields, but it is rarely possible to establish any succession.

The bones of all inhumation burials which are not too badly decayed should be preserved for report. If questions of space or carriage have to be considered, the skull (including jaw), pelvis, and long bones should be preserved, and the rest can be discarded.

VI

The Technique of Field Work:
Recording an Excavation

An excavation, however well conducted, is waste of time unless it is adequately recorded and published, or worse, for evidence has been totally destroyed. Recording includes survey, records of stratification, the relation of finds exactly to these, and photography.

Survey. The principles of archaeological survey are those of surveying in general, which can best be studied in any manual of surveying. All that is attempted here is to give a brief description of those methods most useful on excavations, in order that a beginner who is asked to assist may understand what he is doing, and of the few points which require adaptation for use in archaeology.

The requirements of an archaeological survey are to put the site on the map, to make a plan of the site and its structures, and to show the area excavated.

The first requirement, to put the site on the map, is one that is sometimes overlooked. The problem of doing this in a country of which no accurate large scale map exists is beyond the scope of this book, and we need only consider the case of areas for which large scale maps of the type of the 25-inch or 6-inch Ordnance Survey exist. It is not adequate in such cases merely to record that a site, for instance a Roman villa, is in a particular field, for any future investigator might have considerable difficulty in locating it. It must be accurately fixed so that it can be drawn on the map, and, if it has not got any features which can be readily recognised on the ground, a copy of the relevant portion of the Ordnance Survey,[1] with the site

[1] The permission of H.M. Stationery Office must be obtained for the publication of any maps based on those of the Ordnance survey.

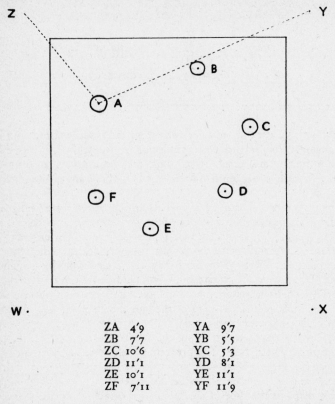

ZA	4′9	YA	9′7
ZB	7′7	YB	5′5
ZC	10′6	YC	5′3
ZD	11′1	YD	8′1
ZE	10′1	YE	11′1
ZF	7′11	YF	11′9

*Fig. 10. Diagram to illustrate survey of post-holes of a hut by triangulating by
measurement from two fixed points.*

added, should be published with the report. The fixing can as a
rule be quite easily done from any two well-defined features on the
map, such as a road junction or angle, a bend of a stream, a field
angle, and so on. These should be related to the survey base line
of the site.

The necessity of making a plan of the site needs no explanation. The purpose of showing the area excavated, including those parts which do not produce any structures is in the first place to show future investigators where it is useless to excavate, and in the second to show that there are definitely no structures in a certain area, for instance in the case of a Roman villa that there are no accessory buildings in that part of the site.

For most types of archaeological sites, a simple form of survey is quite adequate. It can be carried out satisfactorily if a base line is established at some convenient point across the site, from which all other points can be fixed. The line can be established visually by erecting a series of survey poles accurately in line with each other. Then at these points 2 ins × 2 ins wooden pegs should be driven in firmly, with nails in the centres of their tops. The positions of the pegs must be accurately measured, and it is convenient if the measurement of each is painted on it. If required in the course of the survey, temporary intermediate pegs can be established at closer intervals along the base line and their position measured from the nearest peg.

From this base line the structures and other features, and the area excavated, can alternatively be fixed by triangulation or by offsets at right angles. A point can be fixed by triangulation by measurement from two points on the base line, by angle with reference to the base line and measurement from one point, or by angle from two.

For fixing points over a short distance, measurement from two points is the quickest and most accurate. The most convenient way of doing this is to make a sketch plan of the structures to be surveyed, and to letter the points to be fixed. The distance to each can be measured first from one base point and then the other. An illustration and the method of recording is given in Fig. 10. The result should be plotted with compasses and scale while the site is still open so that if the measurements do not work out the error can be traced. It may happen that the base line itself is inconveniently far away from a particular area. In that case, temporary pegs may themselves be fixed by triangulation from the base line, and can in turn be used as the basis for the triangulation of the area in question.

The base pegs used should be so sited that the angle of intersection fixing the points is neither very acute nor very obtuse, since such intersections are not often accurate. A difficulty which may arise in archaeological surveying is when the point to be fixed is considerably below the level of the base pegs, for the tape must be horizontal to be accurate. This can be overcome by holding a plumb-bob over the point, and taking the measurement to its string (Pl. 10). Triangulation by angles can be carried out by any instrument which is capable of close adjustment and accurate measurement of angles, such as a theodolite. A sighting is taken along the base line and then to the point to be fixed, and the angle between is transferred to the plan with a protractor.

A variation of this method is given by the use of plane table and alidade. In this a flat board on a tripod is fixed above a base peg, so that a point on the table is accurately above the peg. The alidade is a ruler with a sight and an aperture with a hair line. This is placed with the sight over the point which is above the base peg, and is first aligned along a base line drawn on the board. With the alidade in this position, the board is then swung round until the alidade is sighted along the base line of the site, thus fixing the position of the board so that the drawn and actual base lines coincide. The alidade is then sighted on the point to be fixed. A measurement is taken to this point, the distance read off on a scale, and the position is thus transferred direct to a scale plan. This method is an excellent one to use in Eastern countries, but has obvious disadvantages in the British climate.

In the course of excavation, the supervisor of a particular area may frequently wish to plan the position of small structures or objects before removing them. It is therefore convenient to have a framework of fixed points from which this can be done. In the section on digging a prehistoric site, the method of a grid with key pegs was described. These pegs should be put on to the plan, so that they can be used for taking subsidiary measurements. In digging a masonry building, the corners of the rooms may be sufficiently well-defined to serve the same purpose—otherwise the necessary pegs should be put in.

In planning a large and irregular structure such as an earthwork, a number of points along it should be accurately fixed, and the intervening areas sketched in by eye.

In Britain, measurements will of course be in feet and inches, but in most Near Eastern countries the metric system is in use. The scale to be used will depend on the size and complexity of the site to be planned. For large buildings, 1/8 inch to the foot, or 1:100 in the metric scale, is probably most convenient, while 1/4 inch or 1/2 inch, or 1:50 and 1:25 can be used for parts requiring greater detail. For a large town area or prehistoric camp, still smaller scales can be used.

The planning of a tell excavation is necessarily more complicated than most British sites, and probably requires the establishment of a grid-plan over the whole site. This is too complicated a matter to go into detail here, and the reader is referred to the Bibliography for a book giving instructions.

Planning on a horizontal plane usually requires to be supplemented by the taking of levels. This is done with a Dumpy level or similar instrument. It consists of a telescope with a fine line across the lens, on a tripod, with an adjustment so that the telescope can be fixed horizontally. This is sighted on a Sopwith staff which is marked in feet and metres. The instrument is set up, and the staff is placed on a base mark. The reading through the horizontal telescope will show the amount the base of the staff resting on the base mark is below the telescope. The staff is then shifted to the first point required. If the reading on the staff is less, the point is higher by the difference between the two readings, if more, it is similarly lower (Fig. 11). If possible, the base mark should be related to a bench mark giving the Ordnance Survey datum level.

There are two main uses of levels on an excavation. The first is for correlating sections and floor levels in different areas. For this it is convenient to have spot levels on a clearly defined point in each area, which will appear in the drawn section. Then, even if two areas have not been drawn on the same section, their relation can be subsequently fixed.

The second use occurs on sites of uneven surfaces such as hill-forts, tumuli and tells, and that is to establish the contour lines.

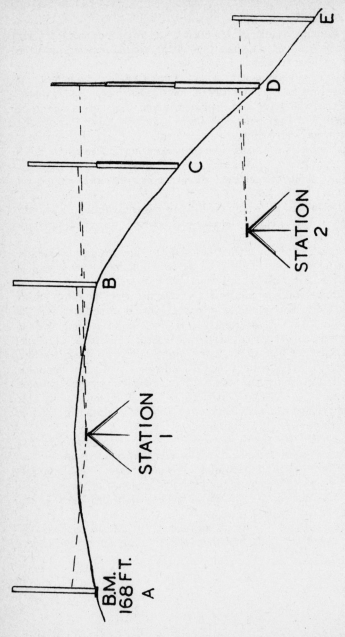

Fig. 11. Schematic diagram to illustrate the taking of levels on a slope with a Dumpy level. The illustration relates the levels to a bench mark of 168 ft, but it need only relate them to an arbitrary one connected with other levels on the site, if no bench mark is available.

	Level at Station	Reading to staff at A, Bench Mark at 168 ft.	Back Reading	Forward Reading	Difference	Result	Notes
1	1	A, Bench Mark at 168 ft.	1.8			168 ft.	
2	1	B		1.4	+.4	168.4 ft.	The staff at B is .4 ft. higher than the Bench Mark.
3	1	C		7.4	—5.6	162.4 ft.	The amount by which the staff at C is lower than the Bench Mark is 7.4 — 1.8 = 5.6.
4	1	D		13.2	—11.4	155.6 ft.	i.e. Level at Station 2 is 11.8 ft. lower than at Station 1. This amount must be allowed for in future calculations.
5	2	D	1.4				
6	2	E		5.4	—4.0	152.6 ft.	Either deduct difference between E & D from actual level of D, 156.6 — (5.4 — 1.4) = 152.6 or deduct sum of difference of 2 stations & reading 6 less reading 1 from Bench Mark, 168 — (11.8 + 5.4 — 1.8) = 152.6.

Notes. As the staff is taken down the hill, a higher point on it is level with the horizontal telescope, therefore a higher reading indicates that the staff is resting on a lower level. The first sight is taken to the staff resting on a fixed point related to the general levels (and/or Ordnance Survey Bench Mark). The difference in reading at the other points shows by how much they are above or below this point. When the instrument has to be moved up or down the slope, the staff is kept at the last point, D on the diagram, at which it was read from Station 1, and the first reading from Station 2 is taken to D. The difference shows how much higher or lower the instrument now is.

The readings are not tabulated here in the ordinary surveyor's method, which can be seen in any book on surveying, but in an expanded form to make the process clear.

This often both suggests the significance of the surface contours, and enables the plan to be much more realistic. The shape of an earthwork, and particularly an entrance, is much more clearly shown by a plan with contours, possibly assisted by hachures, than by any other means. The easiest way to establish the contours is to move the staff so that the reading is constant, and put in pegs at these points. The pegs are then planned, and those of the same level joined up to form the contour lines.

In any large scale taking of levels, it is usually necessary to shift the position of the instrument. To do this, the staff is kept in one position, a reading taken from the old position of the instrument and again from the new. The difference between the two shows the difference in height between the two positions, and this amount must be added to or deducted from subsequent readings in order to relate them to the base mark (Fig. 11).

Records of Stratification. This aspect of recording is of all the aspects the most important for a beginner to understand, for it is his observations as he digs which will form the basis of the record. Details of keeping this record will vary from dig to dig, and a volunteer should of course always follow the method of the person in charge.

The primary record should be kept in a notebook. A convenient form is a Sectional Notebook of quarto size, with the left-hand page of graph paper, and the right hand lined. The graph side can be used for plans, sections and sketches, and notes made on the opposite page. For excavation in this country the graph paper should be in inches and eighths of an inch, and for countries where the metric system is in use, in centimetres and millimetres. On a British dig it is almost essential to cover the outside of the book with American cloth or plastic material, to protect it in wet weather. The pages of the notebook should be numbered. On a complicated site it is convenient to allow several pages of the book to each number, as the complete record will extend beyond one page, and it is more convenient to have the continuation on the following page in the book.

The method of recording an occupation site is rather different from that of the excavation of an earthwork or tomb, and will therefore be dealt with first.

A. Recording Occupation Sites. Each cutting, whether square or trench, should have a numbered page of the notebook. This should be headed by the description of the area. If the site is being dug by the grid system, each square should be lettered or numbered, the former being the more distinctive, as numbers are needed for many other things. On a site in this country, probably a simple letter will be sufficient, e.g. Square A, Square M, etc. On a tell site, it will probably be necessary to letter one axis and number the other, so that the squares will be A1, A5, E10 and so on. In most cases in this country it will probably be sufficient to have one page number to a square. On a tell site there is greater complexity and the size of the square must be greater owing to the depth to be excavated; the square will have to be subdivided and several page numbers allocated to it. The subdivisions of digging will be imposed by the walls encountered. If the area is uncomplicated and on level ground, all visible walls of any one stage may belong to the same period, and the rooms can be numbered and used as the subdivisions. But this is rarely the case. Very often on mud-brick sites, buildings are constructed in a series of terraces. Accidents of survival may leave a wall on a lower terrace and one on an upper terrace standing to the same height, though they may be parts of different buildings and of different dates. The relationship of the walls one to the other often does not become clear until excavation has proceeded further and the full significance of the section can be seen. It becomes very confusing in working out the plan if something has been called a room which never existed as such. It is therefore best simply to designate the area by a page number, and to record in the notebook that it was limited by such and such walls or features. Similarly on a stone-built site, foundations belonging to several different periods may cut down to the same depth, forming entirely artificial rooms, which should be similarly treated.

In any case, all walls should be numbered as they are discovered, as a convenient method of reference. The numbers should be recorded on a sketch plan, and put on the measured plan as soon as this is made.

On a site being explored by trenches, and cleared, if necessary, by using the actual rooms as units, the preliminary trenches can be numbered and noted on a sketch plan. As the structure is traced, the rooms can be numbered (as well as the walls) and the trenches identified in the notebook as 'Room V, N-S, 6 ft east of wall 10'. It is important to record the exact position with reference to some structure which will appear on the plan.

The page having been headed by the description of the area, the layers are recorded as they are dug. They should in the first place be described simply by the kind of soil, or material, e.g. brown gravelly, red clay, or hard mortar surface. As work proceeds and the significance of the layers becomes apparent, this can be amplified, at first as 'Make-up of floor contemporary with wall 6', 'Floor sealing wall 2', etc. Ultimately the ascription to a period or building phase should be added. This is discussed in more detail below.

The layers should be numbered in sequence as digging proceeds downwards. A space of several lines should be left after each entry, both for the amplification just described and for the insertion of subsidiary levels. For instance, in a preliminary trench, level 2 may rest direct on level 3, but at the other side of the square another layer may appear between the two. This is most conveniently called level 2a, and inserted in the space between the two entries. Similarly, there may be a suspicion that part of the area is disturbed, or might include a foundation-trench. The contents of this should be kept separate, and numbered for instance 2b. A specimen page of notebook is shown in Fig. 12. To make the method clear, the first entries are in capitals, while additional ones are not, and annotations and diagnosis are in italics.

The lists of the levels, with their description and diagnosis should be kept as compact as possible, to facilitate future reference. All subdivisions of a level should follow one another in the book, and a reference to level 3, for instance, or a subdivision of it, should not be added after a later level, or much time will be lost when looking up the significance of the level later. If the excavator wants to keep a journal or day-book of the progress of the work, which is sometimes convenient, it should be kept either in a separate book or a separate section of the same book.

The primary identification and description of the levels is made as digging proceeds. But it has already been explained in the chapter on excavation that the method of digging must be such that key sections of the strata are left in each area and against each wall. It is of course essential to be able to identify the layers as described in the notebook with those visible in the section. If the layers are simple and well-defined, this may be easy, but often a succession of rather similar layers makes confusion possible. Two steps should be taken to avoid the possiblity of error. A sketch section should be made on the opposite page as work proceeds, on which should be noted the depth from the surface at which the new levels appear. Secondly, a label or tag should be fixed into the side of the cutting by a staple or bit of wire, with the number of the layer written on it in waterproof ink.

The permanent record of the stratification is made by means of a measured drawing. This is made on graph paper, either in the notebook, if the length of the section is not too great, or on separate sheets. For this is necessary to have a datum for horizontal and vertical measurements. The datum for the horizontal measurements is provided by a measuring tape stretched taut along the face of the section. The datum for the vertical measurements must be horizontal, and it is seldom certain that this is the case with the actual surface. Therefore, a string tightly stretched between two nails or pegs must be adjusted by means of a spirit level so that it is exactly horizontal. It is immaterial where on the face of the section, or above it, the string is fixed, and the most convenient position should be chosen. At given points on the horizontal tape, measurements are taken, with a 5-foot rod or spring rule, upwards or downwards from the string to the surface of the layer being measured (Pl. 11), and these are plotted on the graph paper at the required scale. A minimum scale is 1/2 inch to the foot, or its equivalent 4 cms. to the metre, while if the layers are very complicated it may be necessary to use a scale of 1 inch to the foot or its equivalent. Provided the slope of the layer is fairly regular, it is sufficient to take measurements at intervals of about 2 feet, which can of course be supplemented by other measurements at irregularities or features such as post-holes. A line should be drawn joining up points on the layer as they are plotted. The

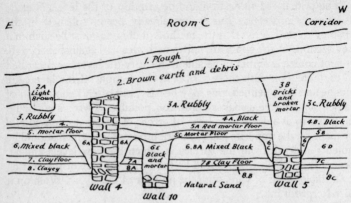

Fig. 12. Specimen page of notebook and accompanying measured drawing of stratification. Capitals represent first entries, ordinary print additional ones, and italics annotations and analysis.

TRENCH 6. 6 ft N. OF WALL I, E—W ACROSS ROOM C.   P.10

PERIODS			FINDS
Mod.	1.	PLOUGH.	
VI	2.	BROWN EARTH & DEBRIS. *Early plough level.*	*Mediaeval sherds.*
Mod.	2A.	Light brown earth. Pit at E. end of trench. Sheep burial at base. Sealed by plough only	
V	3.	RUBBLY SOIL. RUNS UP TO FACE OF WALL 4. *Destruction debris of Period III house.*	*C4 Sherds. I Mediaeval sherd.*
V	3A.	RUBBLY SOIL, W. OF WALL 4. (= 3)	
VI	3B.	Bricks and broken mortar. Cuts down through 3A. from base of 2. *R.T. of Wall 5.*	
V	3C.	Rubbly soil, W. of 3b. (= 3)	
IV	4.	BLACK BENEATH 3. *Occupation on floors of Period III house.*	
1V	4A.	BLACK BETWEEN WALL 4 AND R.T.5. (= 4)	*Coin of Theodosius.*
IV	4B.	BLACK W. OF R.T.5. (= 4)	
III	5.	MORTAR FLOOR. RUNS UP TO WALL 4. *Original floor belonging to wall 4.*	
IIIa	5A.	RED MORTAR FLOOR BETWEEN WALL 4 & R.T.5. *Repair to original floor.*	*Coin of Constantine I.*
III	5B.	MORTAR FLOOR W. OF R.T.5. (= 5)	
III	5C.	MORTAR FLOOR BENEATH 5a. *Original floor.* (= 5)	

PERIODS			FINDS
II	6.	MIXED BLACK BENEATH 5. *Cut by F.T. of wall 4. Accumulation on floors of Period I house.*	
III	6A.	F.T. OF WALL 4.	*Coin of Tetricus I.*
III	6B.	MIXED BLACK BETWEEN WALL 4 AND R.T.5. *As originally dug found to include 6E.*	*Coin of Antonius Pius.*
II	6BA.	Mixed black between Wall 4 & R.T.5, after 6E identified, ∴ pure. (= 6)	*Hadrian-Antonine pottery.*
III	6C.	F.T. OF WALL 5.	
II	6D.	MIXED BLACK W. OF R.T.5. (= 6)	*Coin of Septimius Severus.*
III	6E.	Black with mortar. Cuts down through 6B, from base of 5C. *R.T. of wall 10, robbed when 5C laid down.*	
I	7.	CLAY FLOOR. *Period I floor.*	
I	7A.	CLAY FLOOR W. OF WALL 4. *Runs up to R.T.10.* = 7.	*Flavian pottery.*
I	7B.	CLAY FLOOR, BETWEEN R.T.10 & WALL 5. = 7.	
I	7C.	CLAY FLOOR, W. OF WALL 5. = 7.	
I	8.	CLAYEY, E. OF WALL 4. *Make-up of 7. Overlies Natural Sand.*	*Flavian pottery.*
I	8A.	CLAYEY, BETWEEN WALL 4 & R.T.10. = 8.	
I	8B.	CLAYEY, BETWEEN R.T.10 & WALL 5. = 8.	
I	8C.	CLAYEY, W. OF WALL 5. = 8.	

Diagnosis of evidence (combined with that from other trenches): Period I. House with clay floors and stone walls (if the superstructure to the height of at least 4 ft had not been of stone, it would not have been robbed in Period III). Dated to the Flavian period by pottery. *Period II.* House abandoned. Accumulation of debris and humus. Dating evidence, from pottery and coins, covers second to early third century. Must have been occupation in the neighbourhood to provide this material. *Period III.* New house built. Period I walls robbed. Dated to late third century by coins and pottery. *Period IIIa.* Floor of Room C relaid where had sagged over R.T.10. *Period IV.* Late (untidy) occupation of Period III house. Late fourth century from coins and pottery. *Period V.* Decay and destruction of Period III house. Pottery in fill mainly late Roman (derived from latest occupation), but a little mediaeval. *Period VI.* Mediaeval agriculture, in which remains of house partially removed, in some cases to deep level. Thirteenth and fourteenth century pottery. *Modern.* Plough, and farmer's burial of a sheep.

notebook number and description of the layer should be written on
it in the drawing. As well as the lines of the surfaces of the different
layers, features in them such as tip-lines, piles of stones and so on
should be indicated. The details of any walls included should be
accurately drawn. The course and thickness of mortar joints should
be measured, and the character of the stones, dressed or irregular,
indicated. The drawing should of course make absolutely clear the
existence of foundation trenches, robber trenches, post-holes and
similar features, and their relation to adjoining levels.

A measured section should be made in this way of each area dug
and of the sections against any walls or special features. Provision
must be made for relating up adjacent sections. This may be done
either by running a key horizontal string across the whole area,
which would appear on each section drawn, or by taking spot levels
related to a base level, as described in the preceding section, at some
clearly identifiable point, such as the top of a wall, which appears
on the drawing.

Though in most cases surfaces and layers will run through into
several sections of the dig, and therefore appear on separate pages
of the notebook, it is a mistake to try to give them the same numbers
in different areas. It often happens that intermediate layers, such as
a patch on a floor, an extra layer of filling, or some disturbance, occur
in one area and not in another. Each area should therefore be
numbered independently, and the correlation of the different areas
made subsequently.

This correlation of the layers is an important stage in the interpretation. It is the preliminary to working out the history of the
site. It is not the slightest use digging the layers meticulously and
then not being able to relate the evidence they contain to this history.
The relation of each layer, or group of layers, to the structure must
be established, and the evidence from them can then be used to date
the structure. This is a task in which the utmost conscientiousness
and diligence is required. If a floor stops in mid-air, a reason (e.g.
robber trench, erosion of levels, post-hole) must be found. If a
surface believed to belong to one wall of a room appears to be
earlier or later than another wall, one must not be satisfied until the

reason is found (e.g. the surface is not continuous, or the walls not contemporary). The excavation must be so directed as to provide all the sections necessary to answer these questions, and one must continue to work on them until one is satisfied that one has a watertight answer. The levels of the different stages can then be tabulated as shown in Figs. 13 and 14. Phases should be designated A, B, C, from the top down, until the whole sequence is certain, and then converted in I, II, III, from the earliest upwards.

The preceding paragraphs give the framework within which all finds are recorded. All objects must be so labelled that they can be associated with this record. When digging is in progress, a container must be provided for each level, and this should, as soon as work on a level is begun, be provided with two labels (Pl. 1). These should have on them: (a) the name of the site (a convenient and cheap way of doing this is to have a rubber stamp made); (b) a description of the area, e.g. Square A, Trench 3, or Room IV; (c) a description of the level, e.g. gravel surface, red clay, etc. (it is on the whole safer not to put the ascription to period on the label, e.g. Floor of Period II, since sometimes further work shows a mistake has been made, and confusion may arise when the pottery is being worked over); (d) a short identification which can be marked on the sherds, which is described in the next paragraph; (e) the date; (f) the name of the digger, which is sometimes a useful indication of the reliability of the evidence if any question of contamination arises.

The short identification is essential, since it is necessary to mark all important sherds before they can be freely handled, to avoid risk of mixing them, and the full label would be much too cumbrous and laborious to use. The identification should consist of the initial letter of the site, e.g. V for Verulamium, S.W. for Sutton Walls (it should be remembered that eventually the material may be stored with that from other sites); a letter or page number to show the area, which can conveniently be the square letter on a simple site, e.g. A or Sq. A, but if it is a complex site, with several separate pages to a square, as on a tell site, or to a room, it is better to give the notebook page number; and the level number. A complete example would therefore be V. Sq. B. 6, or S.W. P.10. 2.

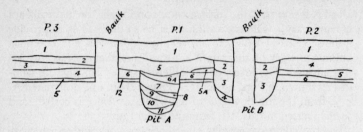

Fig. 13. Diagram to show correlation of notebook levels in adjacent areas on a prehistoric site.

Final Periods	Working Periods		P.1	P.2	P.3	P.4 (Not shown on diagram)
		Plough	1	1	1	1
IIIb	A	Fill of Pit B	2	2		
			3	3		
			4			
IIIa	B	Pit B, cut through Period III hut floor.				
III	C	Floor of Period III hut, overlying Period II hut and Pit A	5	4	2	2
					3	
IIc	D	Upper fill in Pit A	6a			3
			7			4
						5
IIb	Di	Hearth above lower fill in Pit A .	8			
IIa	Dii	Lower fill in Pit A	9			6
			10			7
			11			
II	E	Period II hut, contemporary with	5a	5		
	Ei	Pit A, cut through occupation on Period I hut				
Ia	F	Occupation on Period I hut floor	6	6	4	8
I	G	Floor of Period I hut	12		5	9

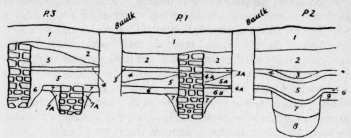

Fig. 14. Diagram to show correlation of notebook levels in adjacent areas on a Roman site.

Final Periods	Working Periods		P.1	P.2	P.3
		Plough	1	1	1
III	A	Destruction debris	2	2	2
					3
IIa	B	Patch above sinkage over early rubbish pit		3	
II	Bi	Floor of 2nd. phase of house	3 3a	4	4
II	C	Make-up and foundation-trenches contemporary with 2nd. phase of house	4 4a 5 5a	5	5 6
Ib	D	Secondary floor of first phase of house, overlying rubbish pit	6a	6	
Ia	E	Fill of rubbish pit cut through 1st floor		7 8	
I	F	Floor and foundation-trenches of 1st phase of house, overlying natural clay	6 6b 7	9	7 7a

This short identification does in fact provide all the necessary information about the find-spot. It is however safer to put the fuller details on the labels, since occasionally in moments of aberration one may write a wrong number or letter, and the description provides a check to them.

It sometimes happens that it is desired to record the position of important sherds more exactly, in fact to pin-point them. This is done by the three-dimensional method of recording, which is described in the section on recording earthworks, since it is the basic method in such digs, and need in fact rarely be used on occupation sites, unless the stratification is not clear as it is dug. It is comparatively rare that the position of sherds in a particular layer within a structure, that is to say a room or a hut, is important. If, however, a group of whole vessels is found, they should be planned, for their position may throw light on the history of the layer or structure.

All objects found should be recorded in the same way. The pottery from each layer should have labels with it, as described, and things like animal bones, architectural fragments, nails and so on may conveniently be put into the same container for the time being. Other objects, such as coins, brooches, ornaments, which can be classed as Small Finds, should as a rule be put straight into boxes or small envelopes. The envelopes should have the same description written on them as the labels, while boxes should have two labels put in them. The use of the two labels in these and the pottery containers is described in the chapter on treatment of finds.

All labels and envelopes should have their descriptions in black Indian ink, which alone will survive wet weather and handling. A ball-point pen is convenient to use, but a special indelible fill must be obtained, since the ordinary one fades badly.

A record has to be kept in this way of each area. The extent to which this record-keeping is delegated depends on the type of dig and the experience of the assistants. On a small dig the director of the excavations will probably keep the record of all areas. But as soon as a dig reaches a size at which he cannot pay close attention to all cuttings, it is necessary to delegate the actual recording to assistants, who will each have their own notebooks, while the director will only check their interpretations and records.

B. Recording Excavations of Earthworks.   The drawing of sections of earthworks can be done in exactly the same way as for occupation sites. Owing to the slope of the ground it may be necessary to use a series of horizontal strings stepped up or down by carefully measured intervals. An alternative method is to draw the surface contour by means of a succession of levels taken with a levelling instrument as described on p. 119. The lines of the strata can then be drawn in relation to the surface contour, by measurement to the surface at each point. The stratification of earthworks is often very complex owing to the number of tip-lines. The significance of the different tips may not be clear until digging has been completed, and it is therefore important to be able to pin-point the finds so that they can if necessary be associated with the correct tip-line. The angle of the tips sometimes makes it very difficult to work exactly to them, particularly if the trench is deep. For this reason, the three-dimensional method of recording is essential to fix the exact find-spot of all objects.

In this method, an object is recorded in its horizontal position by the distance from a datum peg to the point on the side of the trench opposite which it is found, and the distance out from that edge of the trench, and in its vertical position by the depth below the surface at that point in the trench. The datum peg can be driven in firmly at any convenient point, preferably in the crest of the bank. For convenience and rapidity in working, other pegs should be driven in at exact 3-foot intervals from that peg, being placed three-corner-wise, so that the point towards the trench is at the 3-foot mark. When laying them out, the tape should be held horizontal and not along the slope of the ground, which on a steep bank or ditch could cause considerable distortion. The distance in feet from the datum point should be painted on each peg, for ease of reference. All the pegs should be set back 1 foot from the side of the trench. In a very wide trench, pegs should be put in on both sides of the trench.

In order to fix accurately the point opposite which a find is made, a right-angled triangle, with the two shorter arms at least 3 feet in length, should be made. This is placed on the surface against the line of pegs so that the projecting arm is over the position of the object. If necessary, the line of the projecting arm can be prolonged by laying a survey pole along it. By this means the distance along the trench is fixed, the distance of the projecting arm from the nearest peg being measured. By measuring out along the projecting arm to the string of a plumb-bob dropped over the object, the distance from the side of the trench is fixed. Finally, by measuring down from the projecting arm to the object, its depth below the surface at that point can be fixed; for this, it is necessary to have a small spirit level fixed to the projecting arm to ensure it is held horizontally. The process is shown in the Frontispiece.

When the section is drawn with the position of the datum peg recorded on it, the find-spots of the objects recorded in this way can be projected on to it, and thus assigned to the correct strata. The reason for the measurements along the trench and below the surface is self-evident. The reason for the measurement out from the side is that in a wide trench tip-lines sometimes run obliquely and if an object is near the junction of two levels it is necessary to know how far out into a trench the object occurs, in order to be sure to which layer it belongs. In the case of such a trench with oblique tip-lines, it is of course necessary to draw the section of both sides of the trench.

The measurements are most conveniently recorded by the points of the compass. That is to say, if the trench runs north and south, the measurements along the trench would be north or south of the datum peg, the measurements across would be east or west of the line of pegs (depending on from which side of the trench they were being taken), while the depth would be recorded as such. An example would be 32 ft S., 2 ft 6 ins W., 3 ft 9 ins D. The objects should be numbered in sequence, and a register made in the note-book, recording the above particulars, and also the type of layer as an additional check. The register should give a brief description of the find, so that important objects can be quickly picked out. When recorded the object should be placed in a bag with a label with its number and measurements of the find-spot, and the same particulars also written on the bag.

The interpretation of the stratification of an earthwork is on the same principles as that of an occupation site. While the cut is still open, the significance of the different layers must be established.

Their provenance should be deduced, as described on p. 108, and it should be decided which are in fact merely tip-lines essentially contemporary with one another, and which represent later periods. If there is more than one period, the association of any structural features with the different periods must be established. In the case of the ditch, the rapid silt must be identified, and any stages in the filling, such as indications of the collapse of a revetment of the bank, and any evidence of recutting, must be noted.

As mentioned above (p. 132), the same method of three-dimensional recording may on occasion be used on occupation sites, the datum points being provided by the pegs at the corners of squares or trenches.

This method is also the correct one to use for the excavation of tumuli, which from their structure present the same stratigraphical problems as earthworks. The datum peg should be established clear of the tumulus, and the base line would run along the section left standing across the mound.

Photography. The technical principles of archaeological photography are, like those of surveying, exactly the same as those of any other kind of photography, and can be studied in any good manual. All that is attempted here is a mention of some basic elementary principles and a description of the specifically archaeological aspects.

Photographs of an excavation must serve two purposes. They must include general views and important details for the published report, and must provide a record of the appearance of the site, again both general and detailed, during the progress of the work.

General views for the final publication should give as clear an idea of the character of the site and its surroundings as conditions permit. Though the features of the site are the primary consideration, a good pictorial effect is a definite asset, and this is the one kind of archaeological photograph in which an artistic appearance is of real importance. If it is possible, without obscuring the archaeological features, to obtain a nicely balanced composition with the right amount of foreground and sky, well-placed trees, a good contrast of light and shade, the whole effect is much more pleasing. It is also worth while trying to secure good cloud effects. This is the sort of photograph which can probably be taken at any time during a dig, and it is worth taking a number of views under different conditions, from which the most successful can be chosen for publication.

The detailed views for publication should show the general character of the structures, for instance huts, pits, rooms, as a means of illustrating verbal descriptions. They should also include close-up views of details such as wall-construction and post-holes, and of points which provide important evidence for the history of the site, such as the junction of walls or walls cutting through floors. Such photography of evidence is often much clearer than description, and provides visual confirmation that the excavator has not made a mistake. Besides views of structures, there should be close-up photographs of finds *in situ*, for instance burials.

The photographs for record overlap those for publication, for the published photographs are also record photographs. But it is useful to have considerably more photographs taken than will ever be published, as an aid to the excavator's memory when writing the report, and as a means of checking points which may not have been considered while excavation was in progress. For instance, subsequent work on the plan or finds may raise a query as to whether all walls bounding an area were of the same structure, and it is very useful to be able to check this in a photograph. In principle, therefore, it is desirable to have fairly close-up views of all sections of the site.

Though not necessarily every archaeologist can take photographs, all, without exception, should be able to prepare a site for photography. The first essential is that everything should be scrupulously clean. This is necessary not only since the finished result should have a pleasing appearance, which is very important for all photographs which may be published, but also because in a messy photograph important points are often obscured. The edges of all trenches or cuts, and any other edges visible in the photograph, should be straight and sharp. Any dumps of soil should be at least a foot back from the edge of the cut, and trimmed to a line parallel with that of the cut. Grass or weeds along the edge must be trimmed. The angles at the end of the cut should be sharp right angles, and the angle of the face of the cut with the surface at its bottom must be sharp. All surfaces, whether of archaeological levels or the present ground levels must be carefully brushed and must not look smeary or dusty. All walls must be painstakingly cleaned stone by stone and the joints made visible; unless this is done the character of the wall will not be shown by the photograph. Junctions of walls with the faces of cuts or with surfaces must be sharp.

The second essential is that the subject shall be prepared so that the important features show up. Nothing must of course be faked, but a great deal can be done by intelligent emphasizing of points which the photograph is meant to illustrate. A view of a room may be intended to show the general character of the site, which can be emphasized by thorough cleaning and by a choice of view-point showing the shape and size of the room. It may be meant to illustrate similarities or dissimilarities in the different walls and these features should be emphasized in the cleaning, for instance, bonding courses running through adjacent walls, or differences in sizes of stones. If one wall cuts a floor, while others are contemporary, the cut may be emphasized by clearing it slightly below the level of the floor. If a hut floor has to be photographed, it should be cleaned so as to define its edges and any features such as post-holes. For instance, the hard surface of the floor may be swept very clean and smooth, while the softer soil on the line of the wall may be left slightly rough. Sometimes the contrast will be greater if the surface is wet, for the hard surface of the floor will dry more rapidly than the soft surrounding soil. Post-holes can be cleared down so as to show clearly. Any stone features must be carefully cleaned so as to stick up from the surrounding soil, or they will not be well-defined in the photograph.

Soil sections require careful preparation for photography, for it must be remembered that the photograph translates everything into black and white, and differences visible only through colour are lost. The important thing is that any preparation must emphasize existing features and not produce arbitrary differences. One of the most satisfactory ways is to emphasize differences in texture in the different layers. A layer of smooth texture, such as clay, should be cut to a clean surface, which can be smoothed with a trowel. One of rough texture, such as gravel, can have the roughness emphasized by light brushing so as to leave some pebbles prominent. A layer with rubble can have the outlines of stones or debris carefully defined, and dark levels may be slightly damped with a paint brush. Important surfaces can be outlined by slight cutting. For instance, if there is a hard floor level visible in section, the base of the layer above can be slightly bevelled back, so that the edge of the surface catches the light. Any cut through the layers, for instance a posthole, foundation trench or robber trench, can similarly be indicated by emphasizing the texture, supplemented where necessary by outlining. Any outlining, however, should be most carefully done, both to avoid falsifying the evidence and to avoid looking artificial. The only justifiable use of it is to attract the eye to differences which the rest of the visible evidence confirms.

The archaeologist is therefore responsible for the cleanliness and preparation of the subject, though of course if the photographer is experienced in archaeological photography he will be able to give much help in this. The archaeologist is also responsible for seeing that all extraneous objects, such as stray tools, trays of pottery, wheel-barrows and interested spectators, are removed from the angle of vision of the camera. Finally, he must see that a scale is provided, for an archaeological photograph without a scale to convey the size to the eye of the reader of the report loses a large part of its value. The scale can be provided in different ways. For general views, a human figure, or if the subject is a large one, up to three human figures, is the best, for such a figure is easily visible and rather more pleasing to the eye than anything more formal, while an exact measurement, which the human figure cannot give, is unnecessary. Figures used in such a way should be so placed as to help to balance the composition, and of course should not mask important features. They should be naturally posed, not looking at the camera, and preferably appearing to be working.

For medium views, for instance a room, hut, or face of a section, a 6-foot (or 2-metre) survey pole, or sometimes two, marked in red, white and black should be used. This should be so placed as to appear vertical in the photograph (this is discussed below). For small objects, such as a post-hole, or pot *in situ*, a scale 1 foot (or 30 cms.) in length, painted in black and white, should be used.

As has already been said, the archaeologist may not himself take the photographs. This will depend largely on the scale of the dig. On a small dig it is possible for him to do so, but on a large scale one, he is too busy with the responsibilities of excavation to spend the time necessary to take the considerable number of photographs required. It is however desirable that he should at least understand the technique, so as to realise the possibilities and limitations of the camera, and he must always satisfy himself as to the preparation of the subject and the view point, for he alone knows the points to be illustrated.

The principles of photography are comparatively simple, though the practice of course requires considerable experience to produce consistently first-class results. As an introduction, the main principles are described in the following paragraphs, but anyone wanting to take good photographs should go on to read a good manual, and to take practical lessons.

The essential components of a camera in non-technical terms are a holder for the film or plate, a lens which focuses the subject on the film or plate, a light-proof box or hood connecting the two, a diaphragm with a variable aperture which controls the amount of light passing through the lens and incidentally the definition of the subject, a means of controlling the time of exposure, which may be a mechanically operated shutter or a cap removable by hand, and a means of varying the distance of the lens from the film, so as to focus on objects at different distances.

Either plates or films nowadays produce equally satisfactory results, but films of course are much less bulky and heavy, and are almost invariably preferred. Films may be either cut films, carried in holders in the same way as plates, or roll films. The advantage of films or plates in holders is that the holder can be removed and a sheet of ground glass substituted, on which the actual image which will appear in the photograph will be seen. In the ordinary roll film camera, it can only be seen through a view-finder in miniature, which is much less satisfactory, though in an expensive camera of the reflex type a direct view can be obtained, which does not offer the same objection.

The size of the photograph taken of course varies with the camera. Many people today use miniature cameras, from the negatives of which enlargements are made. For some subjects, these may produce excellent results if the camera is a first-class one and its user experienced, but for general archaeological use, a larger camera is to be recommended, of a type which gives direct vision of the subject. For general use, a half plate camera, taking photographs $8\frac{1}{2}$ ins $\times$ $6\frac{1}{2}$ ins, is probably the best, though a quarter plate one, $4\frac{1}{4}$ ins $\times$ $3\frac{1}{4}$ ins, is also very useful.

The lens should be a good quality anastigmat. The lines of light from the subject pass through the curved surface of the lens, being, as it were, collected by it, and then diverge again till they hit the film. In order to form a sharply defined image, the distance of the lens has to be varied according to the distance between the subject and the lens; the nearer the subject, the longer the distance necessary between lens and film. In a direct vision camera, this is obtained by moving the focusing screw until the image is sharp, while in others a scale is provided to fix the position of the lens for different distances.

The diaphragm is a shield which controls the size of the opening through which the light falling upon the lens passes. A lever moves on a graded scale which indicates the size of the opening, or *stop*. Each stop admits half the amount of light of the preceding one, e.g. f.11 half the amount of f.8, f.16 half f.11, and so on. (This numeration is the standard one in Britain; the continental one varies slightly, e.g. f.9, f.12.5, f.18, but the proportions are the same.) At the same time as controlling the amount of light, the size of the stop also controls the amount of definition, the smaller stops increasing the depth of definition by concentrating the image through the centre of the lens. That is to say, with a large stop an object in the middle of the picture will be in focus, while those nearer or further away will be out of focus. With each smaller stop the distance on either side of the central object for which things are in focus is increased, until with the smallest stop the depth of focus is practically from the camera to infinity. In order to see the subject in a direct-vision camera, it is necessary to focus with the diaphragm wide open. The focus should be adjusted so that the most important objects are in focus, and then the diaphragm can be stopped down to a greater or lesser extent according to the variation in distance of the objects to be included. Tables can be obtained which give the depth of focus at the various stops for different types of lens.

The size of the stop obviously affects the amount of the light falling on the film, and therefore the length of exposure. Modern films do allow considerable latitude of exposure within which good results are produced, but at the same time the exposure must be reasonably correct in order to produce good results. An under-exposed film produces strong highlights, but little or nothing in the shadows, that is to say, it has too much contrast. An over-exposed film on the other hand flattens everything out, and has too little contrast.

Three things affect the length of exposure. The first is the speed of the film used. Films (and plates) are accurately graded, mostly to the international scale, which is expressed in Scheiner degrees, e.g. an average speed film is 27° Scheiner. Some firms use their own scale, of which the relation to the Scheiner scale can usually be ascertained. The second factor is the size of the diaphragm, which has already been described. The third is the amount of light reflected from the subject. This is affected by the strength of the daylight which is governed by the clearness or otherwise of the sky, the time of day and year, and the latitude; by the colour and reflective properties of the subject, and by its distance from the lens. Approximate rules can be laid down for calculating these factors of light, and experienced photographers learn to estimate them pretty accurately. But the only safe way, which is almost fool-proof, is to use an exposure meter of the photo-electric cell type. This is especially so in tropical countries, where the variations of light are extreme. There are a number of types of these, but the general principles are the same. The meter is pointed towards the subject, and an indicator records the strength of light reflected. A dial is then adjusted so that this strength is opposite the speed of film being used. Then against any given stop can be read the length of exposure to be given.

The length of exposure may, as has been said, be governed by a shutter mechanically controlled which can be set to a wide range of speeds, or by a cap removed and replaced by hand. For all except the very experienced the former is the only satisfactory way, and is indeed the only possible way in tropical countries, where the strength of light is such that even when the diaphragm is stopped right down, the shortness of exposure is such that it cannot be controlled by hand.

For most archaeological subjects it is best to use a small stop and a comparatively long exposure. This involves the use of a tripod, for a camera cannot be held steady for more than 1/25 sec. Also, the view has to be accurately adjusted, which again involves the use of a tripod. It is worth while getting a well-made one, which will stand really firm, and it should have an adjustable head, preferably on a ball and socket joint, so that the camera can be easily turned and tilted.

A further aid to good photography is the use of filters, and it is by the intelligent use of these filters that clear distinctions can be obtained between stratigraphical layers, while a suitable filter also helps to accentuate cloud-formation. Filters are pieces of gelatine dyed to an international standard of colour, cut and mounted between two pieces of optically ground glass. They are made to fit on the front or the back of the lens. The most valuable types of filters to have for use on the average excavation are: (a) a tri-colour red, (b) a tri-colour green and possibly in tropical countries a pale green filter.

The red and green filters are known as 'contrast' filters, which can be used in conjunction with panchromatic film or plates to obtain a wide variety of contrast between colours which otherwise would be represented by barely distinguishable tones on the photograph. The use of a red filter in combination with the panchromatic material will darken all blues and greens and give extreme lightness in colour to subjects that have a predominance of red, such as dark gravels or sand. In the case of skeletal remains, the red filter will give good sharp distinction between the bones and the earth on which they lie, because the panchromatic film, aided by the filter, absorbs the colour in the bones, thereby making them light and leaving them standing out from the dark earth. With the tri-colour green used again with panchromatic material, the red layers can be made extremely dark. For instance, from a stratified section composed of layers of dark gravel with layers of light sand, the possible result with the correct exposure using a panchromatic film only would be to give an overall sameness (apart from texture) to the section, but if photographed through a tri-colour green the darker gravel would be made extremely dark (owing of course to the non-absorption of the red) and the reflected rays from the yellow sand would be allowed to pass through to give a fairly solid image on the film and consequently an image of light tone on the finished print. For those not accustomed to the use of filters, a glance at the subject to be photographed through the filters will help to decide which to use. It must be borne in mind that the amount of light passing through the lens is cut down considerably by filters, and therefore the exposure will have to be increased. In the case of the red filter the exposure time must be multiplied by four and in the case of the green filter by approximately six. This is a rough guide only, and the definite multiplying factor for each type of film can be obtained from the printed instruction sheet which is usually supplied with it.

The pale green filter referred to earlier, for use in tropical countries, may be kept upon the lens the whole time and with panchromatic material there will be no increase in exposure. It will be found extremely useful as a haze eliminator and as an aid to better tone values where the extreme contrasts given by the red and green filters are not required.[1]

In taking photographs on a dig, the view point has to be carefully selected with reference to the subject and the light. Often there may not be much latitude possible in position with reference to the subject, but it should be carefully inspected through the ground glass screen, or view-finder, from various angles, in order to select

[1] I am indebted to Mr M. B. Cookson of the Institute of Archaeology for these notes on filters.

the best one. It is often necessary to point the camera somewhat downwards in order to include the subject required. In doing this, care should be taken to keep the base of the camera horizontal, and a small spirit level is useful for this. When the camera is pointed down, some distortion is inevitable, since the surface of the film will not be parallel to the surface being photographed. A moderate amount of distortion does not matter, but one adjustment must be made, and that is that the scale should appear vertical on the screen and not to the human eye.[1]

But though there may not be much latitude in choice of position, much may be done by the choice of light. This should be such as to throw important objects into relief. For instance, if a wall is to be photographed, a side light will show up irregularities in the faces of the stones, whereas a front light will flatten them. The subject should therefore be inspected at various times of day, to see which light is best. Deep shadows and a very great range of contrast should be avoided. In tropical countries this often presents difficulties, and it may be necessary to take some photographs about sunrise or sunset. General views often look best taken slightly against the sun, but care must be taken to shade the lens against its direct rays.

Finally, a word must be said about colour photography. As an aid to provide slides for lectures on the excavations, it is excellent, and indeed essential. General views are far more attractive, and details and objects can be illustrated more satisfactorily. But colour photography cannot yet supersede black-and-white for excavation records. In the first place, one must almost always have immediate development in order to check results before the subject is destroyed or lifted. Secondly, if an excavation is deep, as must often be the case on Eastern sites, the colour film cannot yet cope with the range of contrasts liable to be found within the subject. Thirdly, it is still too expensive normally to use colour plates to illustrate archaeological reports. Though black-and-white prints can be obtained from colour transparencies, it is an expensive way to set about obtaining them.

[1] Pls. 7 and 8 are examples of the unpleasing appearance of scales that were placed truly vertical rather than vertical to the eye of a camera looking down.

VII

The Technique of Field Work: Dealing with Finds

In the last chapter, a description was given of how finds should be labelled in the field. Other steps to be taken with them may be conveniently divided into routine treatment of normal finds, and treatment of fragile finds which require special measures. It is most desirable that beginners should be familiar with the routine procedure, for it will save a great deal of the supervisor's time if he has not got to explain all the procedure to all of them.

On most types of excavation the most common normal find is pottery. There are many sites, particularly in the highland zone of Britain, where pottery is very rare before the Roman period. The following description is primarily applicable to sites where pottery and other finds are reasonably common, such as Roman sites in Britain, and Iron Age sites in sourthern Britain. On these sites where finds of all sorts are rare, the arrangements suggested here can of course be considerably modified. The case of sites in the East, where enormous quantities of pottery are found, will require special mention.

On the type of British site described, each digger, or group working together, will require a separate container for finds for each level dug, labelled as already described. These will in due course come up to the dig headquarters. The headquarters will vary with the type of dig. If a room in an adjacent house, with water laid on, is available, it is the ideal arrangement. More often a small hut will have to do. A tent is not satisfactory as it cannot be locked, and therefore finds and tools will have to be taken away each night.

The average group of finds from a level will include potsherds, bones, possibly building fragments such as tiles, nails, shells and so on. They will when found be coated with earth. Diggers should be taught not to try to rub them clean when they unearth them. In the first place, even the stoutest sherd or soundest coin is more tender when first uncovered than after it has had time to dry out. In the second, the earth coating is a good guide to the supervisor as to whether there has been any unintentional or intentional mixing of objects from different layers. The supervisor should frequently inspect each tray of finds, to see what sort of material is being found. If an object has quite different-coloured soil adhering to it, the digger must be cross-examined as to its provenance. If one sherd is dry and the rest all damp, the chances are that it has been knocked out of the side of the cut, or picked up on the surface by an over-zealous workman. In any case where there is the slightest doubt, the object should be discarded, or separately labelled as suspect, rather than risk falsifying the evidence. All diggers must of course be thoroughly drilled as to the importance of putting in the container only the objects from the relevant level.

The treatment when the container is brought up to the head-quarters will vary according to the type of finds. All finds should be left to dry out for a shorter or longer period, according to their soundness. Then good, hard, pottery, such as Mediaeval, Roman, Belgic and most other Iron Age pottery, can be washed. Crumbly Iron Age pottery, Bronze Age, Neolithic and hand-made Saxon pottery should never be washed.

Unless there are insuperable difficulties about water or space, the washing should be carried out on the spot, both because until it is washed the pottery cannot be properly examined, and because if the whole is left until the end of the dig a great accumulation of work is piled up. The washing procedure is simple, but there should be an organised routine. The tray of dirty pottery should be placed on one side of the bowl of water, and a receiving tray on the other. In the receiving tray should be placed one of the labels (weighted if there is a wind!). This is so that if the worker goes away in the middle, none of the finds is left without a label, and is one of the reasons for each group having two labels. Then each object is separately washed and placed in the receiving tray. The whole group should never be emptied into the bowl, both since sherds are apt to be lost and left behind in the silt which soon accumulates at the bottom of the bowl, and since it does sherds no good to have a prolonged soaking. Hard pottery may be washed with an ordinary nail brush, while more doubtful sherds should be washed with a 1-inch paint brush. When the whole group has been transferred to the receiving tray, they should again be transferred to a third, dry, tray, since it is inevitable that surplus water will accumulate in the receiving tray, and make drying much slower. In this third tray the objects are left until they are completely dry.

At this stage it is desirable that the finds should be sorted and selected ones marked. The more sorting that is done on the dig, the easier the task of the person who has subsequently to work over the material. Some objects can be discarded straight away, such as non-significant bones, e.g. ribs, splinters, and long bones without either end. Others can be noted as present in the layer, such as, on a Roman site, oyster shells and fragments of ordinary bricks and roofing tiles. With experience, it is possible to discard a good deal of pottery, particularly on a Roman site. Experience teaches one to recognise when sherds are likely to join to form a repairable pot, and when sherds without rim or base are likely to be of no significance and may be discarded. The more one gets to know the pottery of a particular site and the significance of the different levels, the more one is able to discard. The greater the quantity that one can safely discard on the site the better, for it diminishes the bulk to be carried away, while it is simple to dispose of the discards on the site where they belong, but difficult when away from it, since one is liable to produce problems for future archaeologists, for instance by putting a collection of sherds from Wiltshire in a pit in London.

The material which should not be discarded at this stage includes rims, bases, handles, any sherds significant by reason of their fabric, and any which might repair, identifiable bones, shells other than oysters, nails, and so on. These should be sorted into pottery, bones, metal objects, etc., and each group given its own two labels, copied from the original. If circumstances permit, all rims and bases of pottery, and datable sherds such as Samian, should now be marked with the short identification described on p. 129 (d).

This means that they can be safely handled without risk of information as to their provenance being lost.

The class of finds dealt with in the preceding paragraphs can now be packed. Probably the easiest way to do this is in paper bags of the kind used by grocers, which should be available in various sizes. Some archaeologists, however, prefer cardboard boxes. The bags should then be tied securely with string, all except the tiniest packages having the string round them in both directions and really tight, since otherwise it will slip off in subsequent transport. Before the string is tied one of the labels should be slipped on to it. The string should be tied in a simple, though firm, bow and *not* a reef knot, for it adds enormously to the labour of the person subsequently examining the finds if he has a lot of knots to undo. The second reason for the two labels now appears. It can sometimes happen that the label on the outside of the bag gets torn off; on one occasion an unfortunate mouse got packed in a box, and tried eating the labels and string for nourishment! In such circumstances, the second label inside the bag is a valuable safeguard.

The more fragile kind of pottery requires different treatment up to this stage. It is desirable to clean it to a certain extent on the dig, in order to see what its character is. This may be gently done with a soft brush, once the pottery is quite dry. Alternatively, it may be cleaned with teepol.

It may, however, particularly if it is extremely fragile, be necessary to pack it dirty and deal with it later under laboratory conditions. In any case, it will be necessary to pack it carefully, in boxes and not bags, with a soft packing such as cotton wool, tow, or wood wool. The boxes should, like the bags, have one label inside and one out, and the string tied with a bow.

Having been packed up, the groups must be stored in boxes or other containers. It will depend on the size of the dig how this is done. The larger the dig, the greater the amount of sorting desirable. When there are many finds, there should be separate boxes for bones and miscellaneous materials. Moreover, the pottery should be sorted into separate boxes for each area or cutting, both so that it can be readily referred to again on the dig, and to save time in subsequent work. The boxes should be filled only to the level of the top, so that they can be stacked one above the other, and so that ultimately lids can be put on, if necessary for transport. The boxes should be very firmly packed, so that the bags, if they are employed, will not shake about, for this makes them liable to burst.

So far, only the sort of find which is put in the containers on the dig has been discussed. All special objects, generically classed as small finds, should, as described on p. 132, have been put direct into envelopes; varying sizes of wage or seed envelopes are most useful for this. Larger or more fragile objects should be put direct into small boxes. If this has not been done by the digger, it should be done when the tray comes up for washing.

Most of the objects in this class require laboratory treatment for cleaning if they are metal, or if of material such as bone, can be lightly brushed. In most cases this can well be deferred until after the end of the dig, unless the expedition is exceptionally well-equipped with staff and premises. Coins, once dry, can usually be brushed sufficiently with a tooth-brush to identify the period, at least approximately. The finds should, however, be indexed, and it is desirable, for ease of reference, to do this on the dig. The index should be in three forms: (a) a serial list in numerical order, each piece being given a number; (b) a card headed by provenance and followed by description, with a sketch drawing, which is filed under provenance; (c) a similar card, but headed by description and followed by provenance, which is filed under object, e.g.

SOUTH HILL 10 Sq.A. Brown Clay S.H.P. 1. 5 25.8.50 Bone Pin (Drawing) K. Jones	BONE PIN 10 South Hill Sq.A. Brown Clay S.H.P. 1. 5 25.8.50 (Drawing) K. Jones

These objects can then readily be looked up both as groups from one area, or as groups of the same kind of objects.

The actual way all these various steps are carried out will depend on the amount of material being found, the accommodation available, and the personnel of the dig. If it is possible to have one person completely responsible for the routine, it is the most satisfactory solution. If it is not, all assistants on the dig will have to take their share of washing, marking and packing. In any case, it is probably advisable for all help with washing, for on a prolific dig this may be too much for any one person, and in any case students learn much more about the finds by washing them. On digs not producing much material, and if helpers are few, it is possible to postpone some of the stages, such as marking or indexing, until the material is being worked over at greater leisure.

The finds so far dealt with are the normal type which require no special skill. It does of course often happen that fragile objects are found which require treatment before they can be lifted or handled. Dealing with complicated objects requires special training and technical knowledge, which cannot be dealt with here. A simple treatment alone is described.

The aim of any treatment is to strengthen a fragile object for lifting without risk of disintegration and to prevent decay or distortion. The strengthening agent must be such that it does not damage or discolour the object, and does not interfere with any future laboratory treatment. Paraffin wax successfully strengthens the object, but on many materials it renders laboratory treatment extremely difficult. It may be used on wood but Carbowax 4000 (polyethylene glycol), which is water soluble, is preferable. It is obtainable from Union Carbide Ltd., 103 Mount Street, London, W.1. Wax should never be used on metal or painted plaster, while the method described below is more satisfactory for bone or ivory. In countries such as Britain the objection to many methods has been the difficulty in getting the strengthening agent to penetrate damp material. This difficulty has now been overcome by the use of Vinamul N 9146, diluted with two parts of water to one of Vinamul.

If an isolated object is to be lifted, such as a single bone, it can be freed from the adjacent earth, and the emulsion painted on the surface. It can then be carefully lifted, and the lower part treated. If however an object is to be lifted in a block of earth, such as a complete skeleton of an animal or a badly crushed object, the ground is prepared by isolating the object by cutting a trench round it. This will allow the solvent to evaporate easily and speeds up the drying time, but is not essential. To prevent the escape of surplus liquid, shuttering, standing up some two inches higher than the surface, may be erected round the block of earth, but this is optional. The emulsion is then poured on until no more is taken up. Once this stage is reached, and the evaporation of the solvent has started, the shuttering, if used, can be removed to allow of more rapid drying out.

If the object being impregnated includes a skull or anything with a cavity which may be filled with earth, this method of pouring on the emulsion should not be used, because if the plastic is allowed to run into the cavity and impregnate the earth inside it is liable to make the earth harder than the skull or other object. During transport, movement of this hard block of earth is likely to damage the fragile object. In this case, it is better to apply the emulsion with a paint brush or dropper to the surface of the object only, leaving the earth inside untreated. Several coats of a thin solution are better than one or two coats of a thick one.

If for any reason it is considered undesirable to leave the object exposed in the ground for the length of time necessary to allow a block of earth impregnated with Vinamul emulsion to dry, the block of earth may be lifted untreated, by surrounding it with shuttering and sliding a sheet of metal or plywood underneath. The impregnating can then be done under shelter.

If the earth is reasonably dry, as is often the case in Eastern digs, it is unnecessary to use the Vinamul emulsion. Polyvinyl acetate crystals dissolved in toluol, acetone or alcohol, in the proportion of one cupful of the crystals to four of the solvent, is more satisfactory since they evaporate more quickly than the emulsion. If alcohol is used it should be industrial methylated spirit or some other colourless alcohol of a strength of 80-90%.[1]

---

[1] Vinamul is obtainable from Vinal Products Ltd., Butter Hill, Carshalton, Surrey; polyvinyl acetate from Messrs. Hopkins & Williams, Ltd., Chadwell Heath, Essex; toluol, acetone and industrial methylated spirit from British Drug Houses Ltd., or any other manufacturing chemist.

Metal objects, particularly those of copper alloys and iron, should be dried immediately after excavation, since the presence of oxygen as well as moisture may set up a corrosion process, which has been arrested in the damp but de-aerated soil in which the object was buried. On the other hand, water-logged organic materials, as for example wood and leather, should be kept damp. This can most easily be done by placing them immediately after lifting in a polythene bag, the mouth of which should be tied up tightly. In no circumstances should these materials be allowed to dry before laboratory treatment, since they will invariably undergo a process of shrinking and warping which is irreversible, thus the damage cannot be later undone.

The most difficult problem for the excavator is unquestionably where a metal and an organic material are found combined in a single object, under damp conditions, as for example a metal sword with a wooden scabbard or hilt. When a find of this sort is made, there seems little doubt that the best line of action is to treat it as an emergency and place the object in the hands of a competent laboratory as quickly as possible.

Some aspects of the organisation required to deal with the finds on eastern digs require special mention, largely since the mass of finds, particularly pottery, is so great in eastern countries, and also because conditions of work are somewhat different. As a result, it is in the first place absolutely necessary to discard a considerable amount of pottery. In the second, it is essential to have staff concerned solely with the recording and treatment of finds. Thirdly, the conditions under which permission to excavate is given may require records to be kept in a certain form, and that either all or a proportion of the finds must remain in the country. Therefore, all work of description, drawing and photography must be completed while the dig is in progress.

There are two stages in the discarding of pottery. The groups are brought up from the dig in containers, duly labelled, just as on British digs. They are then washed, and, owing to the bulk of the material, usually placed in orderly groups on the ground or on mats to dry. The responsible archaeologist will probably have to look over these twice a day, and discard all non-significant sherds. Rims, bases, handles and fragments likely to mend are then passed on to the recording staff. Even this much reduced selection may constitute too great a mass to be retained. It is therefore necessary to build up a type series of forms. Sherds can then be recorded as of a particular form in the type series, and if necessary discarded. Such typing must of course only be done by experienced archaeologists. In the case of tombs producing hundreds of vessels, it is sometimes even necessary to discard complete pots, once they have been recorded.

This work in itself makes it necessary to have a full-time recording staff, for those engaged in the actual digging will not have time. The recording staff should include someone trained in drawing objects, and also someone trained in the repair of pottery and simple first-aid treatment of finds, such as cleaning of coins and of objects likely to deteriorate.

Since the conditions under which permission to excavate is granted and also the expense of bringing objects home, may make it essential to leave many of the finds behind, the record must be a complete one. The form of this will probably have to conform with the antiquities regulations of the particular country. The essential from the archaeologist's point of view is that he should have available the information of what objects each area and level contained, and that all identifiable objects should either be drawn (or photographed if more suitable for that) or typed on some drawn object.

It should be taken for granted that every experienced archaeologist should be able to identify, analyse and write up the pottery from his or her dig, or if he is dealing with a stone-using culture, the flint (or other stone) implements. He should also be able to deal with the objects of common use, such as weapons, tools and ornaments. The variety of objects and materials found on the average dig is however such that the excavator cannot be expected to have a specialist knowledge of all of them. What he should know is what objects are important, how to take specimens and whom to consult.

The importance of animal bones as showing the environment and economy of the people being investigated has already been mentioned. Evidence for the environment is also given by the fragments of wood. Wood as such only survives in special soil conditions, but pieces of charcoal are often found and can be identified by an expert. If substantial timbers do survive, for instance in bridge structures, they are useful not only for identifying the timber, but also for the tree-ring evidence. Dating from tree-ring patterns is in a comparatively early stage in this country, though well established in the Americas, and each well-authenticated timber of suitable shape and size helps to add to the evidence.

Shells of mollusca can also be useful for showing the kind of climatic conditions, and these should be submitted for identification. In Chapter III, mention has been made of the possibilities of establishing the type of vegetation, and therefore the climate, by analysing the pollen grains contained in suitable deposits, especially peat. Such analyses are principally important when dealing with the earlier post-glacial periods. It is also possible for experts to determine under what conditions layers, such as turf lines or deposits of silt, were laid down. Deposits inside vessels, or associated with structures, such as tumuli, can also often be identified. In all such cases, it is desirable that the expert should himself see the deposits *in situ*, for he can deduce much that is not apparent to the layman. If it is not possible for him to visit the site, samples should be taken, in clean bags or boxes, and submitted with a full description.

The identification of stones is also important. In the case of ordinary building stone, identification of the source of the stone indicates the resources of the builders, and the amount of organisation required to put up the structure. Stones used in ritual structures may be brought from some considerable distance, since particular types of stones may have had some religious significance attached to them. Objects of stone, such as Neolithic axes, may have been traded over considerable distances, and the identification of the source will help to establish the trade routes. For such objects, the help of geologists should be sought. In the case of prehistoric sites, a geologist should also be consulted as to the type of vegetation the soil is likely to have supported.

In a book such as this, it is impossible to describe all the objects

on which expert reports will help to elucidate the environment
and economy of the settlement being dealt with, but the examples
given will suggest the sort of thing. The subject has been dealt with
in a pamphlet issued by the Council for British Archaeology (see
Bibliography), which also gives guidance as to sources from which
expert help can be obtained.

VIII

Field Work: Field Surveys and Air Photography

EXCAVATION IS THE basic method of investigating the material
remains of the past, and it has therefore been dealt with first. But
important results can be obtained by surface survey. This is the study
of the types and distribution of remains visible on the surface. Such
surveys can be roughly divided into four main classes: the placing
of visible remains on the map, the observation of remains in relation
to their geographical surroundings, the identification of the type of
a particular kind of monument, so that the distribution of the type
can be recorded, and the identification of the period of a site by
surface finds of pottery and other objects.

In Britain, by far the greater number of visible ancient structures
are already recorded on the Ordnance Survey maps. It is comparatively rarely that actual new structures, visible on the ground,
are found, though air photography, which is discussed below, is
constantly discovering new sites. Even in Britain, however, careful
observation may reveal traces of earthworks which have almost
vanished. These may include banks of camps, boundary or running
earthworks stretching across country, sunk roadways, traces of
ancient field systems, and tumuli. The first requisite for anyone
investigating such problems is to obtain a good knowledge of such
earthworks where they are well preserved. Their form, relation to
physical and geographical features, the way vegetation grows on
them and so on should be studied, so that the less well preserved
examples can be identified. One should learn to look at the countryside with an observing eye, and to work out the reason for any
feature which looks as though it is not natural. A bank may be a
defensive work or it may be the edge of an old road worn beneath
the surrounding surface. A ledge in a sloping stretch of ground may

be again the terrace of an old road running transversely across a slope, or a partially filled defensive ditch, or a lynchet formed by ancient ploughing.

Such primitive ploughing tends to work the soil down from the top of the field, thus forming a hollow, or negative lynchet, at the top, and a ridge, or positive lynchet, at the bottom. The tracing of ancient field systems is an important form of field survey, for it throws much light on the contemporary economy. The fields associated with Late Bronze Age and Iron Age cultivation, the latter continuing in some parts of the country through the Roman period, are small and approximately square. They are often connected with sunk roads, or drove ways, and may be centred on a contemporary settlement or camp, which may enable them to be dated. The fields associated with Anglo-Saxon and Mediaeval cultivation are long, comparatively narrow, strips. The difference between the two is due to different methods of ploughing. Traces of such primitive cultivation usually only survive on downland, which was easier to work with primitive ploughs, but has since mostly been given over to pasture as heavier and richer soils were brought into use.

Mounds may be barrows of the various periods, those of long or oval shape being, as described on p. 30, typical of the Neolithic period, while round barrows may be Bronze Age, Iron Age or Roman. They may also be the remains of Mediaeval mottes, or may be the emplacements of windmills. Windmills, moreover, were sometimes placed on the remains of barrows or mottes, as providing ready-made emplacements. The interpretation of the origin of the different types of mounds requires a study of authenticated examples, so that their characteristics can be recognised.

The tracing of lost sections of Roman roads is an outstanding example of what can be done by field survey. The methods have been described in detail by Mr I. D. Margary (see Bibliography) and need not be discussed here.

The technique of this type of survey thus requires in the first instance a knowledge of what the structures in question look like, what is likely to be their relation to physical features such as hill-tops and how the passage of time is likely to have affected them. Secondly, it requires a logical working out of the significance of the visible remains. Thirdly, of course, it requires the ability to put what is observed on the map. In Britain this is comparatively simple, as by the methods described on p. 116, discoveries can be recorded on the 25-inch or 6-inch Ordnance Survey maps. They should then be published, or at least the information forwarded to the Archaeology Officer of the Ordnance Survey.

Such surveys are also necessary in Eastern countries, particularly in the fringe areas, such as the less fertile, and therefore less populated and less known, hinterlands of Syria, Palestine and North Africa. Here, owing to lack of exploration, upstanding monuments may be quite unknown. A survey of the distribution of remains of particular types may throw a great deal of light on the history and economy of the period concerned. An example is recent work on the distribution of fortified Roman farmsteads in the semi-desert areas in the hinterland of Tripolitania, which show how the Roman frontier was defended and the land cultivated, while in the same country a study of the positions of Roman milestones has produced much information about the road system.

In work in such countries, again, the first requisite is training to recognise the type of remains. The mapping of sites identified is not a simple matter as in Britain, for in many such areas no large-scale maps, and often no accurate small-scale maps, exist. It may therefore be necessary to make a complete survey, with theodolite or similar equipment, of large areas, based on recognisable physical features, which can be linked with properly surveyed maps on which archaeological remains can be recorded when these are eventually made.

The field survey of remains in relation to their geographical surroundings chiefly refers to cross-country earthworks, sometimes known as running or travelling earthworks. In parts of Britain there are a considerable number of these travelling earthworks, sometimes quite short stretches, sometimes extending for many miles. In themselves, the majority are undatable. As they were not constructed in connection with settlements, the chance of their containing datable objects is small. Examples which have been dated belong to the Belgic period, the end of the Roman period, the Dark Ages and the Anglo-Saxon period. In most cases they have to be dated by a study of geography in combination with known historical developments. Geographical data must be studied to establish their purpose. They may be intended to form a frontier to a tribal area or kingdom, and their date can thus be suggested from the period in history at which such a boundary would be required. An example of this is the well-known Offa's Dyke forming the boundary between the Welsh and the Anglo-Saxons. Another example is the great dyke between the Belgic oppidum at Wheathamsted in Hertfordshire and Verulamium, which marked the limit of Catuvellaunian territory about the end of the first century B.C. and in which archaeological evidence confirmed geographical probabilities.

Other travelling earthworks were designed to defend vulnerable points in the face of threatened attack. They may be across known roads or tracks, or gaps of open country. All this can be established by a study of the geographical features, in combination with that of the type of soil, from which the prehistoric vegetation can be deduced; this last will show what areas were heavily forested, and often provides the answer as to why the earthworks terminate at certain points. When the purpose of the earthwork has thus been established, history or archaeology may be able to say at what period such defence was necessary. Observation may show that certain existing features were or were not there when the earthwork was constructed, thus providing a *terminus post* or *ante quem*. For example, Wat's Dyke in Shropshire makes use of the Iron Age camp of Old Oswestry, and is therefore not earlier in date than this, though it may of course be, and in fact is, appreciably later.

The field study of the type, within a general class of monument, is of particular importance in connection with barrows, especially round barrows, though it may be useful in connection with many other classes. This is not the place to go into the typology of round barrows, but such monuments are constructed in a number of different ways. A first necessity in working out the meaning of these variations is to study where the different types occur. On the Ordnance Survey maps they are (and can be) only recorded as round barrows, and there is therefore the need for an examination and analysis of the remains on the ground, which has been carried out in great detail in some areas (see Bibliography for examples). Similarly, valuable work can be done by a study of the distribution of different types of hill-forts, e.g. multivallate, with in-turned entrances, and so on (see Bibliography). Much work has been done on various subjects such as these, but there is room for other studies. Once more, the first requisite is a knowledge of previous work and the problems involved.

The identification of the period of a site by surface finds is a type of field survey which is, unlike the last two kinds of survey, more particularly applicable to work in the East than in Britain. On Eastern tells with their prolonged occupation, with cultures rich in objects, particularly pottery, and with a dry surface which tends to be denuded, there are nearly always traces of the pottery and objects belonging to the periods when the tell was occupied. A careful field survey and analysis of the surface finds on the tells can suggest the areas covered by different cultures. The survey may not give complete results, for naturally the majority of the finds belong to the latest period of occupation, but it does give preliminary indications. The results may provide the first knowledge of hitherto unknown cultures, or may indicate the extent of distribution of some already well known.

Field surveys of these types will never provide a full picture, for they deal with surface indications only. Excavation is necessary to supplement them before the full picture can be obtained. But they form an invaluable adjunct to excavation, either as a preliminary in order to obtain a comprehensive view and to select the key points for excavation, or to complete the story and test the results of excavations already carried out. Such surveys are a most interesting form of archaeology. They have the great advantage that they can be carried out with a minimum of expense and equipment. Moreover, they are a form of archaeology in which a comparative beginner can do no damage, for he is not destroying anything. They can only be useful if the person carrying them out has a sound grounding in the book-work of the subject, but if the novice has taken the trouble to acquire this, he need not fear to undertake work on his own, as he should do in the case of excavation.

In the above description of surveys, no mention has been made of air photography, but its use in all types is very great. Everyone nowadays knows that air photographs have contributed enormously to the discovery and elucidation of archaeological sites. Their value is twofold. In the first place, they enable comprehensive views to be obtained which are impossible on the ground, and thus enable the significance of features to be recognised. In the second, they reveal sites and features which are completely invisible on the ground.

Features invisible on the ground may be shown in air photographs in three ways, by shadows, by crop marks, and by soil marks. Almost completely flattened features, such as ploughed-out banks or mounds, may be shown up by air photographs taken with a very low sun; such shadows in most cases are not observed or appreciated when seen from the ground, but become obvious in the comprehensive view given by an air photograph. Crop marks depend on differential growth over underlying features. Over buried walls the crop will tend to be poorer and more stunted, while over the deep soil of a filled-in ditch it will be more luxuriant. Such differences may be so marked as to show up from the mere height of the crop, even as shadow marks. But the differences are much more marked at the time when the crop is starting to ripen, or the grass to become parched. The crop or grass with shallow roots, owing to underlying walls, will turn yellow sooner, and *vice versa*, and if the photograph is taken at just the right moment, will show up clearly.

Soil marks is the term used to describe actual differences in the colour of the soil as revealed when a field is freshly ploughed. For instance, when the material in a bank has been obtained from a ditch which penetrates underlying chalk, traces of the bank can be detected as a band of chalky soil, usually much broader than the original bank because of the spreading effect of the plough.

This description is of course very summary, and the reader is referred to the Bibliography for fuller descriptions.

The uses of air photographs in all types of survey described, and also as an adjunct to excavation, are readily apparent. It is of course an expensive matter to have photographs specially taken, though this can fairly easily be arranged with certain firms which specialise in air photography. Many air photographs do however already exist of areas in this country and overseas, and the best way to find out what exist is to consult local museums and authorities on the subject being studied, while for Britain the Council for British Archaeology may be able to help, and for countries overseas the various British Schools of Archaeology. It is hoped that eventually the very numerous photographs taken for service purposes during the war will be readily accessible, as some already are. For Britain, there is available a complete survey taken at a scale of 1/10,000, prints of which for archaeological use can be obtained through the Council for British Archaeology. These photographs are not taken for archaeological purposes, and may therefore be taken in the wrong light or at the wrong time of year to show up archaeological features; they are also on a smaller scale than is ideal; nevertheless they are worth examining for information.

The correct interpretation of air photographs requires training and skill. Such training should however be considered essential for archaeologists nowadays, for the use of such photographs has added enormously to archaeological knowledge.

A recent development of very great interest is the collaboration between amateur flyers and members of Flying Clubs and archaeologists. Some amateur flyers are glad to direct their flying to a specific object, and there have been a number of examples recently of the valuable work they have done in discovering new archaeological sites and in assisting archaeologists in the elucidation of problems. Fresh developments in this direction can be stimulated in two ways, by interested flyers getting in touch with local archaeologists through the nearest university or large museum, or through the Council for British Archaeology, and by archaeologists seeking to interest local Flying Clubs. Given the establishment of mutual interest, the essential then is that both sides should study the literature (see Bibliography).

CONCLUSION

AS A FOOTNOTE, the following points in the foregoing chapters may be reiterated, for unless the beginner in archaeology has absorbed them, this book will have been of no value.

1. This book is no substitute for practical experience. It is only intended to make the lessons learnt in the field more easily comprehensible.
2. All excavation is destruction, therefore no inexperienced person should undertake it on his own.
3. Excavation, however well executed, without adequate publication is wanton destruction.
4. The principles of excavation here described are those which govern all good modern excavations, though they should be improved upon as archaeological technique steadily advances.
5. The detailed methods of digging and recording here described represent only one of many systems for carrying out these processes. Other schools of field archaeologists have their own specialised methods.

Archaeology is a subject which may offer a career to some, and to some may offer a hobby and a part-time occupation. All can make a real contribution, from the humblest volunteer who digs conscientiously in a hole in the ground to the university professor, and all must start as beginners. The earlier chapters have attempted to show something of the variety of subjects and the different fields of work and method open. There is therefore scope for people with many different interests, turns of mind and physical powers. In particular, for *he* throughout the book should be read *he* or *she*, for there are just as many openings for women as for men.

Finally, *Beginners are welcome.*

APPENDIX I

Bibliography

Note. This bibliography does not pretend to be complete, even for beginners in archaeology. It includes only general introductory works, and those which illustrate particular aspects dealt with in the body of this work. It does not include text-books other than those which are also general works serving to introduce the subject to the student. Periodical publications appear in Appendix V and the reader should note that the excellent *Antiquity* (Newbury, Berks) and *Archaeological Newsletter* (London) are both independent journals.

I am indebted for help in preparing this list to Miss J. du Plat Taylor, Librarian of the Institute of Archaeology, and to Prof. S. S. Weinberg of the University of Missouri, and Mrs S. S. Weinberg, editor of *Archaeology.*

CHAPTERS I-III

V. GORDON CHILDE: *What Happened in History, Man Makes Himself, New Light on the Most Ancient East, Piecing together the Past.*

J. G. D. CLARK: *Archaeology and Society, From Savagery to Civilisation, Prehistoric England, Prehistoric Europe: The Economic Basis, The Mesolithic Age in Britain.*

O. G. S. CRAWFORD: *Man and his Past.*

W. W. TAYLOR: A Study of Archaeology, in *American Anthropologist,* 50.

C. L. WOOLLEY: *Digging up the Past.*

A. V. DE PRADENNE: *Prehistory.*

STUART PIGGOTT: *The Progress of Early Man, British Prehistory, Prehistoric India to 1000 B.C., The Neolithic Cultures of the British Isles.*

SIR CYRIL FOX: *The Personality of Britain.*

C. F. C. & J. HAWKES: *Prehistoric Britain.*

G. E. DANIEL: *A Hundred Years of Archaeology.*

W. M. FLINDERS PETRIE: *Seventy Years in Archaeology.*

STANLEY CASSON: *The Discovery of Man, Progress of Archaeology, Ancient Cyprus.*

C. BREASTED: *Pioneer to the Past.*

R. G. COLLINGWOOD: *The Archaeology of Roman Britain.*

A. GROSE-HODGE: *Roman Panorama.*

G. GLOTZ: *The Aegean Civilisation.*

P. J. H. GOODWIN: *The Loom of Prehistory.*

J. D. S. PENDLEBURY: *The Archaeology of Crete.*

P. NEWMAN: *A Short History of Cyprus.*

W. F. ALBRIGHT: *The Archaeology of Palestine.*

SETON LLOYD: *Foundations in the Dust, Twin Rivers.*

E. Chiera: *They Wrote on Clay.*
R. E. M. Wheeler: *Five Thousand Years of Pakistan.*
H. J. Creel: *The Birth of China.*
J. G. Anderson: *Children of the Yellow Earth.*
M. C. Burkitt: *South Africa's Past in Stone and Paint.*
S. R. Mitchell: *Stone Age Craftsmen.*
G. C. Vaillant: *The Aztecs of Mexico.*
S. G. Morley: *The Ancient Maya.*
P. Kelemen: *Mediaeval American Art.*
P. S. Martin, Quimby and Collier: *Indians before Columbus*
L. S. B. Leakey: *Adam's Ancestors.*
G. H. R. von Koenigswald: *Meeting Prehistoric Man.*
K. M. Kenyon: *Archaeology in the Holy Land.*
I. A. Richmond: *Roman Britain.*

The following are included amongst titles in the series Ancient People and Places: others already published include more detailed studies of aspects or periods; additions to the series appear frequently, and the publisher's list should be consulted (Thames and Hudson).

G. H. S. Bushnell: *Peru.*
S. J. de Laet: *The Low Countries.*
J. D. Evans: *Malta.*
T. G. E. Powell: *The Celts.*
R. Bloch: *The Etruscans.*
R. E. M. Wheeler: *Early India and Pakistan*

CHAPTER IV
J. Johnson: So You Want to be an Archaeologist, in *Classical Journal,* 42

CHAPTER V
R. J. C. Atkinson: *Field Archaeology.*
W. F. Badè: *A Manual of Excavation in the Near East.*
R. F. Heizer: *A Manual of Archaeological Field Methods.*
C. Fox: Two Bronze Age Cairns in South Wales: Simondston and Pond Cairns, in *Archaeologia* 87.
R. E. M. Wheeler: *Archaeology from the Earth, Still Digging.*
S. Piggott: *Approach to Archaeology.*
S. J. de Laet: *Archaeology and its Problems.*

CHAPTER VI
A. H. Detweiler: *Manual of Archaeological Surveying,* American Schools of Oriental Research 1948.
F. Debenham: *Mapmaking.*
Royal Geographical Society, *Hints to Travellers,* 2 vols. 1935-8

A. Frantz: Truth before Beauty or the Compleat Photographer, in *Archaeology* III.

M. B. Cookson: *Photography for Archaeologists.*

CHAPTER VII

Council for British Archaeology: *Notes for the Guidance of Archaeologists on the use of Expert Evidence*, Published by the Council, 1947.

H. J. Plenderleith: *The Preservation of Antiquities*, Museums Association, 1934.

A. Lucas: *Ancient Egyptian Materials and Industries.*

R. S. Forbes: *Metallurgy in Antiquity.*

A. O. Sheperd: Rio Grande Glaze Paint Ware: A study illustrating the place of ceramic technological analysis in archaeological research, in *American Anthropologist* VII.

W. F. Libby: *Radiocarbon Dating.*

W. S. Glock: *Principles and Methods of Tree-Ring Analysis.*

F. E. Zeuner: *Dating the Past, an Introduction to Geochronology.*

K. P. Oakley and C. R. Hoskins: *New Evidence on the Antiquity of Piltdown Man*, in *Nature* CLXV.

I. W. Cornwall: *Bones for the Archaeologist; Soils for the Archaeologist.*

CHAPTER VIII

(The following publications are intended as specimens only of the various types of field survey.)

O. G. S. Crawford: *Archaeology in the Field.*

O. G. S. Crawford and A. Keiller: *Wessex from the Air.*

H. T. U. Smith: *Aerial Photographs and their Application.*

D. N. Riley: The Technique of Air Archaeology, in *Archaeological Journal* CI.

J. Bradford: A Technique for the Study of Centuriation, in *Antiquity*, 1947.

C. Fox, B. H. St. J. O'Neil, W. F. Grimes: Linear Earthworks: Methods of Field Survey, in *Antiquities Journal*, XXVI 1946.

C. F. Fox: *Offa's Dyke.*

I. D. Margary: *Roman Ways in the Weald; Roman Roads in Britain.*

R. G. Goodchild: *The Roman Roads and Milestones of Tripolitania*, Department of Antiquities, Tripolitania, 1948.

R. Braidwood: *Mounds in the Plain of Antioch*, Chicago OIP XLVIII.

British Museum: *How to Observe in Archaeology.*

W. H. Ramsay: *Historical Geography of Asia Minor*, Royal Geographical Society Supplementary Paper IV, 1890.

J. P. Williams Freeman: *An Introduction to Field Archaeology as illustrated by Hampshire.*

C. Fox: *The Archaeology of the Cambridge Region.*

APPENDIX II

University Training in Archaeology

REGULATIONS for admission to study for a first degree vary at the different universities. Details should be obtained from the registrar of the university to which a student wishes to apply. Normally, a certificate of the standard of Matriculation, General Schools Certificate or General Certificate of Education is required, and different universities and faculties require the inclusion of particular subjects in the certificates or taken as additional qualifications. Particulars should therefore be obtained from the university which a candidate desires to attend, at as early a date as possible, to ensure that the right subjects are taken.

In almost all cases in which archaeology is taken as a main degree subject or for a diploma, a reading knowledge of French and German will be required, as original sources in those languages will have to be studied.

At most universities at which archaeology is taught, advanced degrees, M.A., B.Litt., Ph.D. etc., open to holders of first degrees of that or another university, may be taken. Work for these degrees, over periods laid down in the regulations of the individual universities, consists of original research, carried out under the supervision of a teacher of the university, but no course of instruction is provided.

In the following section, details are given of the training at the universities in which archaeology is taught.

OXFORD

As part of course for First Degree

For a Pass B.A. (three-year course, two Public Examinations), the Diploma in either Classical Archaeology or European Archaeology or Anthropology (see below) may be taken in place of two out of the total of three subjects required for the Second Public Examination.

For an Honours B.A. in Classics (four-year course, two Public Examinations):

If Honours are sought in the First Public Examination (i.e. by taking Classical Honour Moderations, a five-term course), it will include a Special Subject (one paper). This, if archaeological, may be either

Homeric Archaeology, *or*

The outlines of the history of Greek sculpture.

In the Second Public Examination (i.e. the Final Honour School of Literae Humaniores, a seven- or eight-term course), an optional Special Subject may be offered by permission (two papers, in addition to the rest of the examination). Subjects include:

Aegean civilisation in the Bronze Age;

Greek colonisation, with a special study of one of the following areas: (a) the West, (b) the Pontus and Propontis;

The history of Greek commerce from 776 to 479 B.C., or from 600 to 403 B.C.;

The history and monuments of the Acropolis at Athens, with special reference to the period from 600 to 300 B.C.;

Greek archaic art from 776 to 480 B.C.;

Greek temple sculpture from 480 to 400 B.C.;

Attic tombstones to the end of the fourth century B.C.;

Hellenistic sculpture;

Greek vases from the Geometric period to the end of the fourth century B.C.;

The development of the Roman frontier defences during the first two centuries A.D.;

Britain under Roman occupation;

The extant remains of the Forum and Palatine, with reference to the history of the period from 49 B.C. to A.D. 193;

Greek numismatics from the origins to 403 B.C., with a special study of either (a) Athens, or (b) Aegina and Corinth, or (c) Ionia, or (d) South Italy and Sicily;

Roman coinage down to the death of Trajan, with special reference to either (a) its political or (b) its historical significance.

Diplomas (open to students of graduate or equivalent status, who must normally be or become members of the University):

(a) *Diploma in Classical Archaeology.* Normal qualification a First or Second Class in either Classical Honour Moderations or Final Honour School of Literae Humaniores. Elementary knowledge of two of the following subjects (one paper each) and advanced knowledge of one other (two papers):

The prehistoric age of Greece, with special emphasis on *either* Minoan Crete *or* Mainland Greece between *c.* 1800 and 800 B.C.;

Greek inscriptions;

Latin inscriptions;

Greek coins;

Greek sculpture;

Greek vases;

Imperial Roman sculpture and coins;

Special districts or sites, to be prescribed or sanctioned from time to time;

The archaeology of Roman Britain (at least one month's excavation advised);

Archaeological evidence for religious beliefs and practices in Ancient Greece;

Greek and Roman painting;

Greek and Roman architecture;

Roman coins from the First Triumvirate to the death of Aemilian (60 B.C.–A.D. 253).

A one- or two-year course. One of the subjects offered must be a Greek one; suitable knowledge of German and of either French or Italian is recommended.

(b) *Diploma in European Archaeology.* Elementary knowledge of the principles and history, methods and techniques of archaeology (one paper), and of European archaeology, from the Neolithic to the age of Greek colonisation and afterwards outside the region of classical civilisation to the ensuing Migration Period (one paper). More advanced knowledge of European Archaeology in one of four periods (one paper) and in one of five regions in that period (one paper). Periods: I. Late Neolithic to twelfth century B.C.; II. Thirteenth to fifth century B.C. (at present this alone is authorised); III. Sixth century B.C. to third century A.D.; IV. First century B.C. to eighth century A.D. Regions: Italy and islands (periods I and II); Central Europe; Gaul and Iberia; British Isles and related Continental coastlands; Northern Europe; Eastern Europe. Also a practical and an oral examination.

A one- or two-year course. Suitable knowledge is required of French or Italian, of German, and of one other relevant language (Latin and Greek included).

(c) *Diploma in Anthropology*. Physical Anthropology, Social Anthropology, Prehistoric Archaeology and Comparative Technology (two papers, essay and practical). with two more papers and practical on whichever of the three is specially studied; also oral examination.

Normally a one-year course.

The Diploma course in Celtic Studies, essentially philological and linguistic, includes Celtic archaeology among the subjects in the optional portion of its syllabus.

Specifically Archaeological Scholarships

There are various post-graduate scholarships mainly confined to classical archaeology; the emoluments vary considerably.

CAMBRIDGE

First Degree

Archaeological Tripos

Part I (taken at end of first year):
1. General Ethnology;
2. Prehistory I;
3. Prehistory II;
4. Physical Anthropology;
5. Social Anthropology;
6. *Either* (a) Comparative Ethnology *or* (b) a special archaeological subject;

7. Essay;

8. Practical examination.

Candidates for Part I shall offer paper 4, 6, 7, and 8 and three papers chosen from among papers 1, 2, 3, and 5.

Part II (taken at end of third year):
  1. History and scope of archaeology;
  2. Methods and techniques of archaeology;
  3, 4. The archaeology of a special area. A pair of papers on one of the following Options:
      (a) The Old Stone Age, (b) Europe, including the British Isles, from the Neolithic to the end of the Early Iron Age, (c) North-western Europe and the British Isles from the beginning of the Early Iron Age to the end of the Viking period, (d) India and the Far East from the earliest settlements to the end of the third century B.C., (e) Egypt and Western Asia, (f) Classical Archaeology;
  5. A special subject in the Option selected for Papers 3 and 4;
  6. Oral and Practical.

Candidates for Part II shall offer papers 1, 2, 5, and 6 and one of the Options (a), (b), (c), (d), (e), or (f).

Part II may be taken in either one or two years by candidates who have either obtained honours in one part of another Tripos or obtained an honours degree in another university.

As part of a First Degree

Anglo-Saxon and kindred studies Tripos

This includes papers containing questions on Bronze Age, Early Iron Age, Romano-British, Celtic, and Teutonic (Anglo-Saxon and Viking) archaeology.

This Tripos may be taken in either one or two years, as either the first or second part of an honours degree course, which would be completed by part of another Tripos. It can also be taken in two years by a candidate who has obtained an honours degree in another university.

Classical Tripos

In Part II of the Classical Tripos (a one-year course for those who
have taken Part I of the Classical Tripos) a candidate may take
either:

Group D (Archaeology):
1. Greek and Roman sculpture and Monument Painting and
   Mosaics;
2. (a) Greek vases, (b) Greek and Roman architecture;
3. *Either* (a) Prehellenic archaeology; *or* (b) Romano-British
   archaeology; *or* (c) the topography, monuments, and
   cults of a prescribed site (or group of sites) of the ancient
   Greek world;
4. *Either* A subsidiary paper in another field of classical studies;
   or three papers in a non-archaeological group (Literature or
   Philosophy or History or Philology).

One subsidiary paper on an archaeological subject, which may
be *either* D1 *or* D3 (a) *or* D3 (b).

Part II may be taken in two years by a candidate who has
obtained an honours degree in classics in another university.

In the Oriental Languages Tripos in Egyptology.

In Part I, taken in second year, from choice of alternatives one of
the following may be taken:
Ancient Egyptian iconography;
Art and archaeology of ancient Egypt.

Post-graduate Diplomas

Diplomas in Prehistoric Archaeology:
1. History and scope of archaeology;
2. Methods and techniques of archaeology;
3, 4. A pair of papers on one of the following options:
   (a) The Old Stone Age, (b) Europe, including the British
   Isles from the Neolithic to the end of the Early Iron Age,
   (c) North-western Europe and the British Isles from the
   beginning of the Early Iron Age to the end of the Viking
   Period, (d) India and the Far East from the earliest settlements to the end of the third century B.C.;

5. Oral and practical.

Diploma in Classical Archaeology:
1. (a) Greek and Roman sculpture, (b) Greek and Roman Monuments, Painting and Mosaics;
2. (a) Greek vases, (b) Greek and Roman architecture;
3. Prehellenic archaeology;
4. Romano-British archaeology;
5. The topography, monuments, and cults of a prescribed site (or group of sites) of the ancient Greek world;
6. (a) Greek Epigraphy, (b) Roman Epigraphy;
7. (a) Ancient coinage, (b) The Construction and Decoration of ancient buildings.

This Diploma is open to:
(i) Candidates who have taken Parts I and II, or either Part I or Part II, of the Classical Tripos. But no candidate who has taken Part II of the Classical Tripos may offer in the Diploma a subject that he has already offered for Part II. Candidates who have taken Group D in Part II shall offer an advanced essay on some subject or combination of subjects studied for Group D, papers 6 and 7, and one paper in each of the two subjects not studied for Paper 3 in Group D;
(ii) any Research Student or Affiliated Student from another university who has satisfied the Faculty Board of Classics of his proficiency in Greek and Latin and who has resided for at least three terms and has received instruction in Classical archaeology under the direction of the Faculty Board during three terms, which need not be consecutive.

Course for No Examination
A general course on Greek and Roman architecture and art (from the Bronze Age to the fifth century A.D.) is normally attended by students reading Part I of the classical Tripos and by students from the School of Architecture and Fine Arts.

LONDON

As Part of a First Degree

For the Final Examination for B.A. Honours (three-year course), the following subjects can be taken:

Anthropology. As one subject out of eight: Archaeological Study of the Development of Culture. As one of four alternative subjects: The Prehistoric Archaeology of a Special Area.

Classics and Latin. As a Special Subject, alternatives include: Greek sculpture, pottery, and vase painting from 800 to 350 B.C.; Civilisation in Greece from 2000 to 600 B.C.—the archaeological material; History and Archaeology of Roman Britain.

Greek. As a Special Subject: first two of above.

Arabic. As an additional optional subject; Islamic art and archaeology.

Geography. As an alternative subsidiary subject: Prehistory of Western Europe.

History, Branch I. As one of ten subjects: The History of the Near East down to 1200 B.C.; The History of the Near East from 1200 to 336 B.C.; The History of the Greek and Roman world down to 336 B.C.; The History of the Greek and Roman world from 336 B.C. to 30 B.C.; The History of the Roman Empire from 30 B.C. to A.D. 64.

As a Special Subject, two papers out of ten, choices include: The History and Archaeology of Roman Britain; Ancient Egypt: The Twelfth Dynasty; Ancient Egypt: The Eighteenth Dynasty.

As an optional subject, choices include: The General History of Ancient Egypt down to the close of the Saite Period; Classical Art and Architecture; Islamic Art and Archaeology.

For the Final Examination for B.A. (General) (three-year course), the Prehistory of Western Europe may be taken as one of the three subjects.

English. As a Special Subject, an alternative is Anglo-Saxon Archaeology.

Hebrew with Aramaic (including Syriac), Hebrew (Ancient and
Mediaeval) with Aramaic, Hebrew, and Arabic, Hebrew and
Assyrian, Hebrew and Egyptian. As an additional optional
paper, choices include: Palestinian Archaeology to 300 B.C.;
The Archaeology of Syria; the Archaeology of Mesopotamia.
In Hebrew and Assyrian, as one of nine subjects, the Ancient
History of the Near East to 330 B.C. In Hebrew and Egyptian,
as one of eight subjects, Egyptian Civilisation to 330 B.C.

Turkish: As an additional optional paper, Islamic Art and
Archaeology.

Post-graduate Diplomas

The courses for the diplomas are open to students of post-
graduate standing, and to students who, though not graduates, have
satisfied the professors in charge of the course that their previous
education and experience qualify them to profit by the course. The
minimum length of the courses is two years, and in some cases
students are recommended to take three years. The courses for the
individual diplomas are given at the different Schools of the University under which they are listed below, and students should
apply to the particular School.

At the Institute of Archaeology, 31–34 Gordon Square, W.C.1:

European Archaeology: A.   Prehistoric Europe;
                       B.1. Western Europe (The Iron Age
                            and the Roman Provinces).

Archaeology of Western Asia: A. Mesopotamia;
                             B. Palestine;
                             C. Syria;
                             D. Anatolia;

Indian Archaeology (in conjunction with the School of Oriental
Studies);

Prehistoric Archaeology.

At University College, Gower Street, W.C.1:
Classical Archaeology: A. Greece;
                             B. Italy to the end of the Republic;
                             C. Roman Empire;

Egyptology.

At the Courtauld Institute:
Chinese Archaeology.

At the School of Oriental Studies, Malet Street, W.C.1:
Islamic Archaeology;
Archaeology of South-East Asia.

Candidates for the Diplomas in European Archaeology (A, Pre-historic, and B 1, Iron Age and Roman), and in Archaeology of Western Asia (B, Palestine), and in Prehistoric Archaeology will be examined in Elements of Technology, Elementary skeletal Anatomy, Elements of Archaeological Technique.

Candidates for the following Diplomas will be required to attend courses in the subjects named: *Classical Archaeology*, *A*, *B* and *C*, Elementary surveying and Elementary architectural and facsimile drawing; *Egyptology*, Elementary human skeletal Anatomy, and Elementary surveying and facsimile drawing; *Chinese Archaeology*, Elementary facsimile drawing; *Indian Archaeology*, Elementary physical anthropology, Elementary surveying and facsimile draw-ing; *South-East Asia*, The History of Archaeology, Archaeological Methods, Elementary surveying, Elementary skeletal Anatomy; *Islamic Archaeology*, Elementary surveying, Elementary architec-tural and facsimile drawing, Elements of Archaeological Technique.

Non-graduate Courses

Non-graduates can in special circumstances be accepted as can-didates for the diplomas as stated above. Other students can as a rule be allowed to attend the lectures for the courses without regis-tering as candidates for the diplomas.

Courses are provided at the Institute of Archaeology in the Conservation of Archaeological Objects, in Archaeological Photo-graphy, and Archaeological Draughtsmanship. No previous qualification is required of candidates. A certificate is awarded to students who have completed the course to the satisfaction of the instructor.

Extra-Mural Course

The University Extension Diploma in Archaeology provides a four-year scheme of study for persons who desire to pursue the study of the subject to an advanced level. No prior qualification is required of those attending the Course, and the Diploma does not have an academic status. It provides an excellent training for those only able to attend evening lectures and for those who have not the necessary qualifications to take a Post-Graduate Diploma.

The scheme of study is as follows:

First Year: Aims and Methods;
Second Year: Archaeological History of Civilisation, Part I;
Third Year: Archaeological History of Civilisation, Part II;
Fourth Year: Intensive study of one of the following options—

(a) Geochronology and Palaeolithic;
(b) Prehistoric Britain;
(c) Roman Britain;
(d) Post-Roman Britain and Mediaeval Britain.

Annual examinations are held on the year's work. Students are urged to participate in practical field work at an approved excavation for at least a fortnight during the four years of the course.

Specifically Archaeological Scholarships

Douglas Murray Travelling Scholarship in Egyptology of £42 awarded triennially. Margaret Murray Prize in Egyptology of £20 awarded triennially.

BELFAST
The Queen's University

As part of a First Degree

As part of B.A. course (three years):

As subsidiary subject, one-year course on British archaeology of prehistoric and historic times up to the eighteenth century; two papers in examination.

As part of Celtic Honours Course, lectures and examination in third year in Celtic archaeology.

As part of B.Sc. course (three years):

As subsidiary subject, one-year course, to be taken not before second year, preceded by Geology I, on British archaeology, with special emphasis on the contribution of the techniques of the natural sciences, with practical work in the latter; two papers in examination.

Course of lectures on the Archaeology of the Christian era is taken by History Honours students.

Remarks

Students have opportunities for training in fieldwork in connection with the Archaeological Survey of Northern Ireland, which works in association with the Department of Archaeology of the University.

BIRMINGHAM

Archaeological subjects in which a First Degree can be taken
For B.A. with Honours in Ancient History and Archaeology

The Course includes instruction in the following fields:

(a) Ancient History (Classical);
(b) Classical Archaeology;
(c) British and European Archaeology (including early medieval);
(d) History and Archaeology of the Near East.

During the first two years of the three years' work, selected periods and subjects from all these fields will be studied. In the third year Honours candidates will specialise in one of the four fields mentioned above.

As part of a First Degree

For B.A. Honours, archaeology may be taken:

As a subsidiary subject (one- or two-year course) in degrees in English, French, Italian, Geography, and Philosophy;

As a Special Subject (one-year course) in Classics and History.

For the General Honours B.A., Archaeology may be taken:
   as a main or subsidiary subject (one-, two- or three-year
   course).

Non-graduate courses
   Advanced study groups are held under the joint aegis of the
Department of Ancient History and Archaeology and the Extra-
Mural Department. The Extra-Mural Department also organises
Sessional Courses. A speciality of the Extra-Mural Department is
residential courses, normally of two weeks' duration, in archaeological field-work. Elementary, Intermediate, and Advanced
courses on the Roman site of Viroconium are ordinarily held each
summer vacation, and a course on an Iron Age site may also be held.
Students for these courses are housed at the Field Studies Centre
at Preston Montford, near Shrewsbury. Students need not be
members of the university. Early application is advisable.

DURHAM
Durham, and Kings College, Newcastle upon Tyne
As part of a First Degree
For a B.A. Honours course (three years):
   In History, courses on the history and archaeology of Roman
      Britain and on Roman provincial administration (2 papers and
      a dissertation in final examination);
   In Classics, as an optional Special Subject,
      at Durham, course similar to that in history (2 papers in final
         examination),
      at Newcastle, course on the history of the Roman frontier in
         the North of Britain (one paper in final examination);
   In English, course on Anglo-Saxon England;
   In Classical Hebrew and Old Testament Studies,
      at Durham, a compulsory course (one paper in final examina-
         tion) on the History of Palestine from the earliest times to
         63 B.C., with a general study of Hebrew civilisation, and as
         one out of seven Special Subjects, Palestinian archaeology

with a special study of the Lachish, Samaria, and Jericho
sites (one paper in final examination);
In Ancient Egyptian and Nubian Studies,
    at Durham, a compulsory course (one paper in final examina-
tion) on the History of Egypt from the earliest times to the
conquest by Alexander, and a general study of Egyptian
civilisation;
In Classical Chinese Studies,
    at Durham, a study of history and archaeology is included.

EXETER

As part of a First Degree
For a B.A. Honours (three-year course):
    In History, as an optional 'Aspect' in Part I, British Prehistory,
one examination paper, and as an alternative Special Subject
in Part II, Roman Britain, two examination papers;
    In Classics, as an alternative Special Subject in Part II, Roman
Britain, one examination paper;
    In Geography, British Archaeology can be selected as an Addi-
tional Subject in Part I; two examination papers: British Prehistory and Principles and Methods.
For a General Degree (three-year course)
    British Archaeology can be taken as one of three subjects: Part I,
two papers: British Prehistory and Principles and Methods;
Part II, two papers: Roman Britain.

KEELE

University College of North Staffordshire

As part of a First Degree
    Courses in Roman–British and Greek Archaeology are provided.

LEEDS

As part of a First Degree
Honours or Pass degrees may be awarded in either Special or
General Studies Schools.

In the Special Studies School of Greek, as a Special Subject (one out of seven options):
Greek sculpture, *or* Vase painting, *or* Epigraphy;
Greek art and architecture.

In the Special Studies School of Latin, as a Special Subject (one out of six options):
Roman life and manners (with some reference to inscriptions);
Roman art and architecture;
History and archaeology of Roman Britain.

In the Special Studies Schools of Classics and of Latin with Greek the options given in the two previous Schools are also available.

In the Special Studies School of Semitic Languages and Literatures a course on Biblical History and archaeology is compulsory. As a subsidiary subject, one out of six options is Palestinian Archaeology.

In the Special Studies School of English, Anglo-Saxon art and archaeology may be selected as a Special Subject (one out of twelve options) by candidates specialising in philology and medieval literature.

In the Special Studies School of History, the History and archaeology of Roman Britain may be selected as a Special Subject (one out of ten options).

In the Special Studies School of Philosophy with History, the same subject as in History may be selected.

In the General Studies School, students who follow one-year or two-year courses in Hebrew also study archaeology.

LEICESTER

As part of a First Degree
For B.A. Honours (three-year course):
In History, as a Special Subject, two papers out of nine; The History and Archaeology of Roman Britain.
For B.A. General:
First-year course in Prehistoric, Roman, and Anglo-Saxon Britain, and archaeological methods and techniques;

Second-year course in advanced methods and techniques and
either Late Bronze Age and Iron Age Britain *or* the Civil
Settlement of Roman Britain.

LIVERPOOL

Archaeological Subjects in which a First Degree can be taken
For B.A. Honours—B.A. in Special Studies (Oriental Studies):
four year course. *Egyptology:* Ancient Egyptian Language and
one other ancient Oriental Language (either Coptic or Hebrew,
or exceptionally Assyrian or Classical Arabic); History of Ancient
Egypt; Archaeology and Literature of Ancient Egypt and of the
additional oriental language).

As part of a First Degree
B.A. in General Studies (three year course; Honours may be
awarded on combined results of the Second and Third Year
Examinations. Eight courses must be offered over the three years,
and of these one subject at least must be studied for three years;
it is also permissible to study two subjects for three years each).

  (a) Subjects in which three year courses may be offered:
      Ancient Egyptian Language;
      Egyptian Archaeology;
      Classical Archaeology (Greece or Rome).
  (b) Prehistoric Archaeology may be offered in General Studies
      as a one-year course only—and in almost any other degree
      course in the Faculty of Arts.
      Archaeology of the Celtic Peoples may be taken as a
      subject in the Celtic Language course.
  (c) Classical Archaeology may be offered as part of the B.A.
      in Special Studies (Classics).
A course on the archaeology of the Celtic peoples is available to
honours students in Celtic Languages and on the Teutonic
peoples to honours students in German, English Language,
and History.

Post-graduate Studies
Post-graduate Diploma in Archaeology. Two-year course on

Principles and Methods, and study of a special area, selected from: Ancient Egypt, Greece and Rome, Prehistoric Western Europe and the British Isles, or such other areas as may be approved.

Graduates of recognised universities may pursue research studies for the degrees of M.A., and Ph.D., in archaeological subjects within the Departments of Egyptology, Classical Archaeology, and Prehistoric Archaeology. These Departments possess excellent research libraries.

Non-graduate Certificate

Certificate in Archaeology. One-year course in Principles and Methods, and Outlines of culture and civilisation of a special area, as above.

Specifically Archaeological Scholarships

T. E. Peet Travelling Prize. Nominally £150. Open to graduates. Awarded every fifth year, in Egyptian language and Egyptology or the Prehistory of the Mediterranean lands and/or the Near East.

MANCHESTER

As part of a First Degree

For General Degree of B.A.:

Ancient History I (i), Near Eastern Archaeology;

Ancient History II (i), Near Eastern Archaeology;

Ancient History II (iii), Prehistory of Britain.

For B.A. Honours (three-year course):

Ancient History II (iii), Prehistory of Britain, may be taken as one of the subjects in Part II of Honours History;

Archaeology of Roman Britain may be taken in Part II of Honours Classics and Honours Latin.

READING

As part of a First Degree

As a Special Subject, one paper only, for B.A. Honours in Classics, Latin and Greek (two-year course), the following subjects may be taken: Greek vases, Greek Sculpture, Roman Britain.

Specifically Archaeological Scholarship

R. P. Austin Travelling Scholarship, £35. Awarded triennially.

SOUTHAMPTON

As part of a First Degree

In History, tuition includes visits to local archaeological sites, and importance is laid on the use of archaeological evidence in suitable connections;

In Classics, a study of archaeology is required for part of the General Paper (one out of eight papers). The options for the Special Subjects include Greek Art and Architecture and The Roman Provinces, with special reference to Britain.

EDINBURGH

Archaeological subjects in which a First Degree can be taken

For the Honours M.A. (four-year course; no B.A. degree is available at Scottish Universities), Prehistoric Archaeology may be taken as the principal subject, with five subsidiary subjects, of which two are up to Intermediate level. The final examination includes, besides set papers, a short thesis.

For the Honours B.Sc. (four-year course), Prehistoric Archaeology may be taken as the principal subject.

As part of a First Degree

For an Ordinary M.A. (three-year course), Prehistoric Archaeology may be taken as one of seven subjects (two-term course), with two examination papers.

Classical Archaeology, covering either the outlines of Greek Archaeology *or* the outlines of Roman Archaeology, may be taken as a main Special Subject (two examination papers, the second being a special subject or site) or as a subsidiary Special Subject (one paper).

For an Honours M.A. in Classics (four-year course), courses are given in Greek and Roman sculpture, Greek and Roman architecture, Greek vase-painting and Roman Britain. Ancient History and Antiquities is a compulsory subject and Classical Archaeology may be studied (one out of four options) as a Special Subject. Students are encouraged to visit museums and to take part in approved excavations.

ST ANDREWS

As part of a First Degree
For Honours M.A. in Classics (four-year course) Classical Archaeology is an option.

UNIVERSITY OF WALES

University College of South Wales and Monmouthshire, Cardiff

Archaeological subjects in which a First Degree can be taken
For B.A. Honours (three-year course), Archaeology may be taken as the principal subject (with two other subjects in the first year).
As part of a First Degree
For B.A. Pass (three-year course), Archaeology may be taken as one of two principal subjects (with one other subject in the first year and one auxiliary subject in the second year).
For B.Sc. Pass (three-year course), Archaeology and Geology may be taken as principal subjects (with one other subject in the first year and either Botany or Zoology in the second year).
For B.A. Honours Greek, Greek Archaeology (one-year course) may be taken as an alternative Special Subject.
For B.A. Honours Latin; Roman Britain (one-year course) may be taken as an alternative Special Subject.

University College of North Wales, Bangor

As part of a First Degree
For B.A. Honours in History, a course on the Archaeology of Prehistoric and Roman Britain may be taken as a two-year accessory course (one paper in final examination).

NATIONAL UNIVERSITY OF IRELAND

University College, Dublin

As part of a First Degree
For B.A. Honours (two years, after passing First Arts Examination):
In Celtic Studies, Archaeology may be taken as one of the Special Subjects, in the second and third year;

In Architecture, Archaeology is a subject of the Second University examination.

For B.A. Pass, Archaeology may be taken as one of three subjects, for two years.

Post-graduate Course

The M.A. (minimum course, three terms) may be taken in subjects dealing with Irish or British Prehistory.

University College, Cork

As part of a First Degree

Pass and Honours Archaeology may be selected as a subject for the First Arts Examination (one-year course).

For B.A. Honours (two-year course after passing the First Arts Examination), Archaeology may be selected as one of two principal subjects, during the second and third years.

For B.A. Pass (two-year course after passing First Arts Examination), Irish/British Prehistory, with the European and Eastern background, may be taken as one of the three main subjects.

Post-graduate Course

As for Dublin.

University College, Galway

As for Cork.

Specifically Archaeological Scholarship

A Travelling Studentship in Archaeology is offered for competition every three years amongst graduates of the University (from all three Constituent Colleges) of not more than five years standing. Present value of the Studentship is £600 per annum, tenable for three years.

TRINITY COLLEGE, DUBLIN

As part of a First Degree

For B.A. Honours

For honours and professional students, Irish Archaeology can be taken as a subsidiary subject.

In Hebrew and Oriental Languages, Hebrew Archaeology can be
taken as a subsidiary subject.

University Training in Archaeology in the United States and Canada

The training for professional competence in any phase of archaeology is provided largely by Graduate Schools, although many
universities and colleges offer excellent undergraduate curricula as
well for the preliminary training of archaeologists. However, the
student who has decided to become an archaeologist before he
enters university or college is still rare; some make this decision
during their undergraduate years, but to many it comes only at the
end of this period. For those who make the choice early, there are
excellent opportunities at almost any school to take certain preliminary training which will prove most helpful both for graduate
study and for the actual practice of archaeology in the field. To this
end there is suggested here a list of undergraduate subjects which
will be taken with great advantage by anyone aspiring to a career in
archaeology, in the field, in research, or in teaching.

A reading knowledge of French and German is required for advanced degrees in most universities; it is necessary for research
work in most phases of archaeology. Other languages are obviously
necessary for certain special areas, as for instance Spanish for some
American archaeology, Greek and Latin for Classical archaeology,
Hebrew for Biblical archaeology, and these can usually be studied
in the undergraduate years. Egyptian, Hittite, Assyrian, etc., are
more often graduate subjects, but in some schools these, too, can be
started earlier.

Ancient History in general, and the history of various regions of
the ancient world in particular, is essential, as are History of Art and
of Civilization. General Anthropology and Ethnology are both
helpful background subjects.

Among the sciences, Geology is most important for the archaeologist; the Geography of special regions is useful. A first course in

Human Anatomy is important. Physics and Chemistry form a
necessary background for one interested primarily in the preservation of antiquities, Botany and Zoology for those interested in
Palaeontology and Palaeobotany, all important aids to the archaeologist in the field and in the laboratory.

Very useful and important tools can be acquired in first courses
in Freehand Drawing, Draughting or Architectural Drawing,
Surveying and Plane Table Mapping, Ceramics. A knowledge of
Photography is essential and can be obtained in or out of school. It
has aptly been suggested that even a course in Journalism provides
a useful tool for the archaeologist, for the results of excavation are
sterile until they are published.

It should be clear, then, that great advantage accrues to the student
who, deciding early on an archaeological career, can profit by taking
as many of the above courses as possible during his undergraduate
years, before the pressure of acquiring the special knowledge of any
particular field precludes such border studies. Late comers into
archaeology will of necessity pick up the knowledge they require in
any of these subjects as best they can. Many of the specialized jobs
in the field will be done by special technicians, such as architects,
artists, photographers, anthropologists, chemists, geologists, soil
scientists, but not every expedition can command the services of
all the specialists it needs, nor are they always available at the proper
moment and in the right place; a little fundamental knowledge on
the part of regular staff members, resulting from the undergraduate
training suggested here, can prove most fortunate.

After receiving a college degree, the student's problem is to
choose the Graduate School which offers training most suited to
his needs and interests. It is at this point that he will have to make
a definite choice of his main field of specialization; at least, he must
choose between the eastern and western hemispheres. Later, he will
be able to define his interests more closely.

A list is given herewith of the major institutions which offer
graduate work in various fields of archaeological research. Since the
requirements and the courses tend to vary from year to year, no
detailed information concerning these can profitably be given here.

It is suggested that the student contemplating graduate work in archaeology consults the catalogues of a number of institutions (their location will doubtless play some part in the choice) and select the one which best conforms to his needs and interests.

Most of these institutions offer graduate scholarships and other aids. A few have fellowships for travel abroad; these are for students who have already made progress toward an advanced degree. Not all the institutions listed below offer the Ph.D. degree.

American Archaeology

The opportunities for studying American archaeology, especially that of North America, are of course quite extensive. Advanced degrees are generally offered in the Departments of Anthropology, and considerable work in the latter field is usually required. Practically all the institutions listed below offer field work, that is, actual practice in excavating. A few institutions conduct excavations in Middle and South America; the student whose interests lie in that field will have a narrower choice than the one interested in the archaeology of North America. It may also be noted that many universities in Central and South America, as well as those of Canada, specialize in the archaeology of their own regions.

Major Institutions offering Graduate Work in American Archaeology:

Alaska, University of	Florida, University of
Arizona, University of	Georgia, University of
Arkansas, University of	Harvard University
Beloit College	Indiana, University of
Brigham Young University	Kansas, University of
British Columbia, University of	Kentucky, University of
California, University of	Michigan, University of
Chicago, University of	McGill University
Colorado, University of	Minnesota, University of
Columbia University	Mississippi, University of
Denver, University of	Missouri, University of

New Mexico, University of
North Dakota, University of
Ohio State University
Oklahoma, University of
Oregon, University of
Pennsylvania, University of
San Francisco State College
Southern California, University of

Stanford University
Texas, University of
Toronto, University of
Utah, University of
Washington, University of
Wisconsin, University of
Yale University

Classical Archaeology

A fairly large number of institutions offer graduate work in Classical Archaeology. Degrees are generally awarded in the Departments of Classics or of Art, and the student will be obliged to pursue studies in at least one of these related fields. In only a very few universities are degrees offered in classical archaeology alone.

Major Institutions offering Graduate Work in Classical Archaeology:

Brown University
Bryn Mawr College
California, University of
Chicago, University of
Cincinnati, University of
Columbia University
Cornell University
Harvard University
Johns Hopkins University
Michigan, University of
Mississippi, University of

Missouri, University of
New York University
North Carolina, University of
Oberlin College
Pennsylvania, University of
Princeton University
Stanford University
Toronto, University of
Washington University
Yale University

Near Eastern Archaeology

A full programme of study in the field of Near Eastern archaeology is offered by only a few institutions, but many have courses in the languages and history of the Near East, and supplementary instruction (particularly in Biblical archaeology) can often be obtained at theological schools (for example, at McCormick Theological Seminary if the student is pursuing a course at the University of Chicago).

Major Institutions offering Graduate Work in Near Eastern Archaeology:

Chicago, University of	Michigan, University of
Columbia University	Toronto, University of
Harvard University	Pennsylvania, University of
Johns Hopkins University	Yale University

Far Eastern Archaeology

Studies in this field can be pursued at a limited number of institutions, and courses in the language and history of Far Eastern countries can be found at a few others.

Major Institutions offering Graduate Work in Far Eastern Archaeology:

California, University of	Michigan, University of
Chicago, University of	Pennsylvania, University of
Columbia University	Toronto, University of
Harvard University	Washington, University of
Hawaii, University of	Yale University

(specializes in Polynesian archaeology)

European Archaeology

The Departments of Anthropology in most institutions offer survey courses in European prehistory. Perhaps the most complete programme in this field is offered at Harvard University.

APPENDIX III

British Schools of Archaeology

FIVE British schools of archaeology have been established, at Athens, Rome, Jerusalem, Baghdad and Ankara, at which students can gain first-hand knowledge of the archaeology of the country in which they are interested, and at which more senior scholars can have facilities for research. The schools are intended primarily for postgraduate students, but others can sometimes be accommodated at them for short periods. The staff of the schools will give guidance to students in the subjects of their studies, and will of course give every assistance in making the necessary arrangements, but specific courses of instruction are not arranged. Students are expected to have sufficient grounding in their subjects to be able to pursue their studies without detailed supervision. The schools are thus centres of research rather than of instruction.

The schools were all established by private enterprise, and until comparatively recently depended entirely upon private subscriptions. Modern conditions have made it necessary to apply to the Treasury for subventions, which are made in recognition of the valuable work done by the schools in promoting international scholarship and relations. The management of the schools remains, however, in the hands of their governing bodies, and private support is still very necessary.

British School of Archaeology at Athens

The School was founded in 1886 to provide British students of the literature, art, archaeology, and history of Greece of all periods from the earliest times to Byzantine and modern days with facilities for research and travel in Greece. Students of other subjects have also been assisted from time to time.

Archaeological staff. Director and Assistant Director.

Accommodation and facilities. The School maintains a hostel in

Athens, at which there is an extensive library. The hostel is open from 1 November to 30 June each year. Students are given facilities for using the Greek public libraries, and for using the libraries and attending the lectures of other foreign schools, and the Greek Archaeological Service grants free access to museums and excavations.

Students. The following studentships are offered:

School Studentship offered in alternate years to duly qualified members of the Universities of Oxford and Cambridge; value £75, to be made up to £200, if necessary; minimum period of residence three months.

Macmillan Studentship offered when funds are available to graduates with Honours degree in Classics; tenable for two consecutive sessions; value £250 p.a. (made up to £400 in recent years).

Sachs Studentship offered every three to four years to a graduate of a university within the British Isles; value £150; minimum period of residence three months.

Students are required to pursue a definite course of study.

Graduate holders of travelling studentships, etc., of all universities of the British Empire and of other learned bodies are accepted as students. Members of other British schools can usually be accommodated for short periods, and applications from other qualified persons are considered.

Excavations. Work in the field has always formed an important part in the activities of the School. Excavations are carried out on sites on the Greek mainland and in Crete. Many of the students of the School assist at the excavations.

Publications. The School publishes *The Annual of the British School at Athens* and an *Annual Report*, also (in conjunction with the Hellenic Society) *Archaeological Reports*.

Address. Enquiries and applications for admission should be addressed to the Secretary, British School at Athens, 31–34 Gordon Square, London, W.C.1.

British School at Rome

The School was opened in 1901. It consists of Faculties of Archaeology, History and Letters, of Art, and of Architecture. Students in all these subjects are accommodated at the School. Details concerning the Faculty of Archaeology, History, and Letters only are given here.

Archaeological staff. Director and Librarian.

Accommodation and facilities. The School maintains a hostel in Rome, at which there is an extensive library. The hostel is open from 1 September to 30 June. Students can make use of the facilities afforded by the public museums and libraries in Rome and elsewhere in Italy, and of those of other foreign schools. They can obtain free access to museums and excavations.

Students. The following scholarships are offered annually:

Rome Scholarship in Classical Studies awarded for research in ancient history, antiquities, or literature of some period before A.D. 330.

Rome Scholarship in Medieval and Renaissance Studies awarded for research in Medieval and Renaissance history, antiquities, and literature (within the period A.D. 330–1550).

Both Scholarships are awarded for one year, but scholars may apply for election to a second year; maximum value £350 p.a., but less than the maximum may be awarded if the scholar has emoluments from other sources; the scholar must work in Rome, or other approved place abroad, for at least six months in each year.

Riviora Scholarships or Grants for work in Medieval Archaeology are awarded from time to time. The candidates must be graduates of Oxford or Cambridge.

Scholars must pursue a definite course of study, a scheme for which must be submitted with applications.

Other duly qualified students can as a rule be accommodated at the School. During the summer vacation, when the School is open in the month of September, short-term visitors with approved qualifications, such as teachers of classics, are welcomed.

Excavations. The School has recently carried out excavation and survey in South Etruria and in Libya.

Publications. The School publishes an annual volume of *Papers of the British School at Rome.*

Address. Enquiries and applications for admission should be addressed to the Secretary, British School at Rome (Faculty of Archaeology, History, and Letters), 1 Lowther Gardens, Exhibition Road, London, S.W.7.

British School of Archaeology in Jerusalem

The School was founded in 1919, to further studies in the archaeology, history, and topography of Palestine. Activities were suspended between 1939 and 1951. In 1952 excavations were re-sumed in Jordan, and in 1956 a School building was re-opened in Jerusalem, Jordan.

Archaeological staff. Director (part-time) and Secretary-Librarian.

Accommodation and facilities. The School building in Jerusalem accommodates the full-time students of the School. Visiting scholars and students can stay at the School if space (which is limited) permits. Owing to the frontier regulations between Jordan and Israel, which permit only a single, one-way transit, students working in Israel would not be able to stay at the School. The School possesses a good library on the archaeology of Palestine and the neighbouring countries, and students are also able to make use of the libraries of the other archaeological Schools in Jerusalem and of the library and collections of the Palestine Archaeological Museum.

Students. An annual scholarship of £375 is offered to graduates of universities of the British Commonwealth for research in Palestine on an approved subject; a period of residence of eight months is normally required. An excavation scholarship of £175 is offered annually to enable the holder to participate in the School's excavations.

Excavations. The School organises each year one or more excavation campaigns, in which students of the School participate. In addition to those holding scholarships awarded by the School, other students who can obtain funds to travel to Jordan can usually be accepted, and their living expenses while working on the excavations can be paid.

Publications. The *Bulletin* of the School is combined with the *Palestine Exploration Quarterly* of the Palestine Exploration Fund.

Address. Enquiries and applications for admission or accommodation should be addressed to the Secretary, British School of Archaeology in Jerusalem, 2 Hinde Street, Manchester Square, London, W.1.

British School of Archaeology in Iraq

The School was founded in 1932, as a memorial to Gertrude Bell. Its interests cover the whole field of Mesopotamian archaeological and linguistic studies. Besides conducting its own excavations, the School gives assistance to scholars interested in all branches of Mesopotamian history, literature, and art.

Archaeological staff. Director (part-time) and Secretary.

Accommodation. The School maintains a hostel in Baghdad, open from September to May, at which students can be accommodated. The climate of Baghdad is too hot for residence during the summer months to be advisable. A library is housed at the hostel.

Students. The School offers annual Fellowships, which are intended more especially for senior students. Occasionally grants may be made to assist junior students. No conditions are made as to length of stay in Iraq. Students of archaeology visiting Baghdad can stay at the School in so far as accommodation is available, and help can be given to them in arranging their programme by the staff of the School.

Excavations. The School conducts excavations in Iraq normally each year in the spring months. Students can participate in these excavations and receive training.

Publication. The School publishes *Iraq* twice yearly.

Address. Enquiries and applications for admission should be addressed to K. H. J. Hayes, Esq., the Hon. Secretary, British School of Archaeology in Iraq, 5 New Square, Lincoln's Inn, London, W.C.2, or to Miss G. C. Talbot, Assistant Secretary, British School of Archaeology in Iraq, Institute of Archaeology, 31–34 Gordon Square, London, W.C.1.

British Institute of Archaeology at Ankara

The Institute was founded in 1948 to provide a centre of archaeological research in Turkey for students from Great Britain or the British Commonwealth.

Archaeological staff. Director and Assistant Director.

Accommodation and facilities. The Institute maintains an establishment in Ankara, consisting of a library and hostel, which remains open from 15 March until 15 December each year. The hostel provides temporary living accommodation for those members of the Institute officially registered as 'students' or 'senior students'. Such members are also afforded facilities for cheap travel and assistance in obtaining the official permits necessary for work on ancient sites and in museums.

Students. The Institute offers annually a Fellowship, value £350, and a Scholarship, value £300. Such students are required to pursue a pre-arranged course of study, and the minimum period of residence required is three months.

Excavations. The Institute maintains a programme of excavations, which consists of a main project in charge of the Director and occasional subsidiary enterprises conducted by the Assistant Director and others. Places on the staff of excavations are sometimes available for students, but priority in this respect is given to those subsidised by the Institute itself.

Publications. The Institute publishes annually a journal called *Anatolian Studies* and a series of *Occasional Publications* on specialist subjects.

Address. Enquiries and applications for studentships should be addressed to the Secretary, British Institute of Archaeology at Ankara, 16 Bryanston Street, London, W.1.

American Schools of Archaeology

There are six American Schools of Archaeology, which serve as centres for the training of American archaeologists and for the conduct of excavations in various parts of the world. They are primarily postgraduate institutions and, for the student who has made some progress in a particular field, a year or more spent at one of these Schools is the best possible training obtainable. As a resident at an American School, he will have the opportunity to study the material in which he is interested and often to take part in excavations. None of these Schools awards degrees, but academic credit for time spent there can usually be arranged with the institution in the United States from which the student has come.

In their administration and their work the Schools are independent of each other, and their programmes vary. Starting with the oldest, the Schools are:

American School of Classical Studies at Athens. Founded 1881.
The School was established in order 'to give to qualified students the opportunity of studying the antiquities and art, the topography, the history, the language, and the literature of Greece; to prosecute and aid original research in these subjects; and to conduct exploration and excavation of ancient sites.' The School has an excellent library (as well as the Gennadius library, which covers the mediaeval and modern fields) and a residence building with accommodations for students. To qualify for admission, a student must be a graduate of some American college or university. He is expected to have a knowledge of classical Greek, although exceptions are occasionally

made if the student is otherwise well qualified. The course of instruction includes trips conducted by staff members to the major archaeological sites and to many minor ones. lectures on the topography and monuments of Athens, as well as at the museums. During the spring term each student either participates in an excavation or prepares a paper as the result of original research. Opportunity is given to attend lectures and courses offered by the other foreign schools, and students have the privilege of using the libraries of these schools.

There is also a Summer Session, independent of the regular session, which is open to graduate students and to undergraduates who have completed the junior year. In a six-week course they study the monuments of Athens and visit the major archaeological sites on the mainland and the islands. The course is extremely useful for those who cannot spare a full year for study in Greece. Grants for study at this session are offered to teachers by regional classical associations.

The School offers two fellowships in archaeology, at present awarded on the basis of academic records, written work, and letters of recommendation. For information concerning these, and the School in general, address the Secretary of the Managing Committee, Prof. Charles A. Robinson, Jr., Brown University, Providence 12, R.I.

The School publishes a quarterly journal, *Hesperia*.

American Academy in Rome. Founded 1894.

In the School of Classical Studies, a division of the Academy (which also has students in Architecture and other branches of the Fine Arts), a course is offered similar to that outlined in connection with the Athens School. The emphasis is, of course, on the archaeology and monuments of Italy. The Academy has an extensive library and a residence hall for students. The School also conducts excavations in which qualified students may take part. The year's programme usually includes a conducted trip to Greece. There is also a Summer Session, similar in programme to that of the Athens

School, and grants are available to classics teachers who wish to take this course.

Fellowships at the Academy are awarded on the basis of academic record and scholarly work, For information concerning the Academy address the Executive Secretary, Miss Mary T. Williams, American Academy in Rome, 101 Park Avenue, New York 17, N.Y.

The Academy publishes *Memoirs*, also *Papers* and *Monographs*.

American Schools of Oriental Research. School in Jerusalem founded 1900. School in Baghdad opened 1923.

The American Schools of Oriental Research were founded 'to promote the study and teaching and to extend the knowledge of Biblical literature and of geography, history, archaeology, and ancient and modern languages and literatures of Palestine, Mesopotamia and other Oriental countries, by affording educational opportunities to graduates of American Colleges and Universities and to other qualified students and by the prosecution of original research, excavation and exploration'.

The building of the Jerusalem School, which includes a library and residential quarters, is situated in what is at present the Hashemite Kingdom of Jordan. A regular course is offered, including lectures, seminars, and field trips to historical sites and areas. Students may also take part in excavations conducted by the School. To qualify for admission, students must be graduates of accredited colleges or theological seminaries. Students are not accepted for less than a full academic year.

The School in Baghdad has as yet no building of its own, but research facilities are provided at the Iraq Museum, where the library of the School is housed, and members may take part in research and excavation.

Several fellowships are available at the Schools, some to predoctoral candidates, others to those having the doctoral degree. Information concerning these and admission to the Schools may be obtained by writing to the President, Prof. A. Henry Detweiler, Cornell University, Ithaca, N.Y.

The Schools publish the *Bulletin*, the *Biblical Archaeologist*, and the *Annual*.

School of American Research. Founded 1907.

The headquarters of the School are at Santa Fe, New Mexico, where it maintains offices, laboratories, a library, and a museum. The School's activities are mainly in the field of research. For information, address the Director, Dr Wayne L. Mauzy, Palace of the Governors, Santa Fe, N.M.

The School publishes a monthly periodical, *El Palacio*.

American School of Prehistoric Research. Founded 1921.

The School conducts research and excavations, but at the present time offers no courses for students. Besides its headquarters at the Peabody Museum of Harvard University, it has an office in Algiers and recently has been engaged in excavations in that region. For information address the Director, Dr Hugh Hencken, Peabody Museum, Harvard University, Cambridge 38, Mass.

American Research Center in Egypt. Founded in 1948.

The Center conducts research in Egyptology and Islamic Studies in Egypt. For information on fellowships and current activities, address the Secretary, Mrs Elizabeth Riefstahl, P.O. Box 27, South Essex, Mass.

APPENDIX IV

Posts in Archaeology

A. Civil Service

THE functions of the three branches of the Civil Service which deal with archaeological matters are described in Chapter IV.

Recruitment for the Inspectorate of Ancient Monuments and Historic Buildings, for the Royal Commissions and for the posts of Archaeology Officers of the Ordnance Survey is by advertisement and open competition. The Civil Service Commissioners, who are responsible for the recruitment, give notice of vacancies in the Press, and those interested have to apply for entrance forms and particulars. Candidates are required to supply details of their training and qualifications, and to give the names of referees for qualifications and character. Candidates are then interviewed by a selection board. Posts are open to both men and women. Vacancies do not occur at any regular intervals, as they depend on promotions and resignations and retirements within the branches. Those appointed to established posts are eligible for pensions when they retire.

The present establishment and salaries of the three branches are given below. The salaries given are the national rates for men. In addition, officers serving in London are paid a London Weighting according to salary. Women receive slightly lower salaries but will receive equal pay by 1 January 1961.

Inspectorate of Ancient Monuments and Historic Buildings, Ministry of Works (under the Chief Inspector)

Grades of personnel	Present salary scale	Present numbers
Assistant Inspector, Grade II	£635 to £1120	7
Assistant Inspector, Grade I	£1210 to £1600	8
Inspector (of whom two receive an allowance of £205)	£1265 to £1865	8
Assistant Chief Inspector	£1265 to £1865 plus £340 per annum allowance	1

Candidates must be between 23 and 30 years of age. Qualifications required are an Honours Degree, and an enthusiasm for, and some knowledge of, archaeology, especially of the Mediaeval period. Promotion to the grade of Inspector is by merit and according to vacancies.

The Headquarters of the Inspectorate is in London, but officers are also stationed at Scottish Headquarters, Edinburgh, and Central Office for Wales, Cardiff. Three of the posts of Assistant Inspector are in Scotland and one in Wales. The posts involve a considerable amount of travel about the country.

Royal Commission on Historical Monuments (England)

Grades of personnel	Present salary scales	Present numbers
Investigator	£635 to £1120 ⎫	Combined com-
Senior Investigator	£1210 to £1600 ⎬	plement of 15
Principal Investigator	£1265 to £1865	8

Candidates must be at least 21 and under 35 years of age. They must satisfy the Civil Service Commissioners that they have received such systematic education and possess such knowledge as to fit them for the post. Those holding a university degree or corresponding qualification will be given preference. A knowledge of the history and practice of English architecture is necessary.

Royal Commission on Ancient Monuments (Scotland)

Grades of personnel	Present salary scales	Present numbers
Investigator	£635 to £1120 ⎫	Combined com-
Senior Investigator	£1210 to £1600 ⎬	plement of 3
Principal Investigator	£1265 to £1865	2

Candidates must be at least 22 years of age; the upper age limit is subject to adjustment. The qualifications of candidates are not stereotyped, but some of the posts are filled by architects, not archaeologists.

Royal Commission on Ancient Monuments in Wales & Monmouthshire

Grades of personnel	Present salary scales	Present numbers
Investigator	£635 to £1120 }	Combined com-
Senior Investigator	£1210 to £1600 }	plement of 4
Principal Investigator	£1265 to £1865	2

Candidates must be at least 21 years of age; there is not at present an upper age limit. Candidates should normally have a first or second class Honours Degree, but candidates without this qualification may be accepted if otherwise exceptionally well qualified. Up to two years increments may be given for post-graduate work, and a further two for service in the armed forces. Candidates must have a knowledge of architecture, the history of applied art, or the archaeology of Britain. Knowledge of Welsh is not essential, but of two candidates with otherwise equal qualifications, the one with a knowledge of Welsh would be preferred. Any competent Investigator can rely on promotion to the Senior Investigator Grade. About one-third of the working time of the staff is spent in examining monuments in the field. The small number of the staff makes it necessary for each investigator to be capable of dealing at least with the minor monuments of all periods, whatever his own special interest.

Archaeology Branch, Ordnance Survey

Grades of personnel	Present Salary scales	Present numbers
Assistant Archaeology Officer	£1210 to £1600 (personal to present holder)	1
Archaeology Officer	£1265 to £1865	1
Draughtsmen and Surveyors		
Class IV	According to age At 21 from £415 to a maximum of £820	32
Class III	£820 to £975	12
Class II	£975 to £1160	2
Class I	£1160 to £1410	1

The Archaeology Officers are recruited in the same manner as for other Civil Service posts. The Draughtsmen and Surveyors are recruited from these grades within the general staff of the Ordnance Survey. Those showing an interest in and aptitude for archaeological work would stand a good chance of appointments to this Branch, after their initial training in drawing and surveying. Vacancies for Draughtsmen and Surveyors in the Ordnance Survey are advertised in the Press, and appointments are made by examination and selection. The examination is in mathematics, geography, English, and general knowledge. Candidates must be between the ages of 16 and 25. The Headquarters of the Archaeology Branch are at Chessington, Surrey.

The Archaeological Survey of Northern Ireland

Grades of personnel	Present salary scales	Present numbers
Principal Inspector	£1265 to £1865	1
Senior Inspector	£1210 to £1600	1
Archaeological Adviser to the Government of Northern Ireland	Post held in conjunction with University Readership	1

B. University Posts

Provision of teaching posts in universities varies from time to time. At universities at which archaeology is only a subsidiary subject, it may be taught by those holding posts in classics or ancient history, if the existing holders are interested in the subject. If they are not, special appointments may be made. Again, a teacher of archaeology at a university may be given the status of Reader or Professor in recognition of personal distinction, but there may be no permanent post of that class. Temporary appointments for particular purposes, such as junior demonstrators, registrars of collections and cataloguers may be made from time to time. The following list can therefore only give an indication of present posts.

Applications for vacancies are usually but not invariably invited by advertisement in the Press. In other cases, the field of possible candidates, particularly for more senior posts, is so well known that no advertisement is issued. Salaries are at the usual university rates. Holders of permanent university posts participate in a superannuation scheme.

Oxford

Professorships	Classical Archaeology and Art (Lincoln Professor);
	European Archaeology (Neolithic to Early Mediaeval);
	Archaeology of the Roman Empire;
	Egyptology;
	Keepers in the Ashmolean Museum (Departments of Antiquities and Numismatics) have the equivalent of Professorial rank.
Readership	Classical Archaeology.
Senior Lectureship	Mediaeval Art.
Lectureships	Near Eastern Archaeology (in the Faculty of Oriental Studies);
	Ancient Numismatics (two, part time, held by staff of Ashmolean Museum Coin Room);
	Homeric Archaeology (part time, held by a College Tutorial Fellow in Classics);
	Greek Epigraphy (part time, held by a College Tutorial Fellow in Classics);
	Mediaeval Archaeology (part time, held by a College Tutorial Fellow in History).
Research Assistantship	European Archaeology.

Cambridge

Professorships	Classical Archaeology (Laurence Professor);
	Prehistoric European Archaeology (Disney Professor);
	Anglo-Saxon and Kindred Studies (Elvington and Bosworth Professor);
	Egyptology.

Readership   Classical Archaeology (Laurence Reader).
Lectureships   Classical Archaeology;
                    Prehistoric European Archaeology (four
                        Lecturers);
                    Anglo-Saxon Archaeology;
                    Near Eastern Archaeology (two Lecturers);
                    Far Eastern Archaeology (two Lecturers).

London
Professorships   Classical Art and Archaeology (Yates
                        Professor);
                    Prehistoric European Archaeology;
                    Egyptology (Edwards Professor);
                    Western Asiatic Archaeology;
                    Indian Archaeology;
                    Chinese Archaeology;
                    Environmental Archaeology;
                    Islamic Art and Archaeology;
                    Ancient Semitic Languages and Civilisa-
                        tions.
Readerships   Archaeology of the Roman Provinces;
                    Egyptian Archaeology.
Lectureships   Palestinian Archaeology;
                    Western Asiatic Archaeology (part time);
                    Egyptology;
                    Environmental Archaeology;
                    Prehistoric European Archaeology;
                    Prehistoric Archaeology;
                    Archaeology of South-East Asia.

Belfast
Lectureship   Archaeology (at present combined with the
                        post of Archaeological Adviser to the
                        Government of Northern Ireland).

Birmingham
Readership   Ancient History and Archaeology.
Lectureships   Ancient History and Archaeology;
                               Egyptian Art and Archaeology;
                               History and Archaeology of the Near East.
Assistant Lectureship   Ancient History and Archaeology.
Technical Assistant   Photography and drawing.

Durham
Professorship   Roman–British History and Archaeology
                               (personal appointment, not chair). At
                               Durham.
Readership   Roman–British History and Archaeology.
                               At Newcastle.
Lectureship   Anglo-Saxon Antiquities and Archaeology,
                               Roman–British History. Duties at Dur-
                               ham and Newcastle.
                               Teaching in oriental archaeology is given at
                               Durham by the Professor in Semitic
                               Philology, the Reader in Egyptology, the
                               Lecturer in Hebrew and the Lecturer in
                               Chinese Language and Civilisation.

Exeter
Lectureship   British Archaeology (part time).

Leeds
Lectureship   Romano–British Archaeology.

Leicester
Lectureship   British Archaeology.
Assistant Lectureship   British Archaeology.

Liverpool
Professorship   Egyptology.
Lectureships   Senior Lecturer in Prehistoric Archaeology;
                         Lecturer in Classical Archaeology;
                         Egyptology.

Manchester
Professorship   Ancient History.
Lectureship   Archaeology.
Assistant Lectureship   Near Eastern Archaeology.

Edinburgh
Professorship   Prehistoric Archaeology (Abercromby
                             Professor).
Lectureships   Prehistoric Archaeology;
                         Classical Archaeology.

St Andrews
Readership   Classical Archaeology.

Cardiff
Professorship   Archaeology.
Lectureships   Archaeology (two).
Technical Assistant

Bangor
Lectureship   Archaeology.

Ireland, National University of
Professorships   Celtic Archaeology. At Dublin.
                         Archaeology. At Cork.
                         Celtic Archaeology. At Galway.

Trinity College, Dublin
Lectureship   Classical Archaeology (Louis Claude Purser
                             Lecturer).

C. Museums

Appointments to the National Museums are made by the Civil Service Commissioners in the same way as to other archaeological posts in the Civil Service. Vacancies are notified in the press, and selection is on qualifications and by interview. Candidates must have an Honours degree, normally with First or Second Class Honours unless they have additional qualifications. Candidates are not necessarily expected to have had prior training in the subject which is dealt with by the department for which they are applying. Candidates for senior posts must ordinarily be between the ages of 22 and 25. Other Civil Service conditions, such as superannuation, also apply.

Other museums are run by local authorities, universities and archaeological societies. The conditions vary so greatly that it is impossible to generalise as to staff, salaries and qualifications required. Appointments to museums run by local authorites are subject to annual increments, superannuation schemes etc., but since the status and scope of the museums vary greatly, there is no fixed starting rate.

Vacancies are advertised in the Press and the Museums Journal. Those interested in obtaining a museum post should get in touch with the Museums Association, Meteorological Buildings, Exhibition Road, London S.W.7.

American Posts, Fellowships and Scholarships

Posts

The opportunities for a professional career in archaeology in the United States vary considerably according to the field of the archaeologist's specialization. Naturally, they are far greater for the expert on American archaeology than for those in other fields, for the Americanist has numerous opportunities in both Federal and State positions. These are, for instance:

Federal Government: Under the United States Civil Service Com-

mission, there are a number of posts in American Archaeology
(Classification—Archaeologist, GS-193-0). The positions include
those of Curators of Archaeology in the Smithsonian Institution
and the National Museum, Senior and Junior Archaeologists in
each region of the National Park Service and in each of the River
Basin Surveys. Trained archaeologists are also eligible for posts
under the classification of Museum Art Specialist. For full particulars address the U.S. Civil Service Commission, Washington 25,
D.C.

State and City Governments: A number of states have·State Archaeologists in charge of field work and the administration of their
antiquities acts. Many also have State Museums in which curatorial
and research posts are open to American Archaeologists, and there
are many municipal museums in which posts may be obtained.

Universities: For the specialist in American Archaeology, as well as
for those trained in Classical, Near Eastern, Far Eastern, European,
Prehistoric, or any other field of archaeology, there are teaching
positions in American universities and colleges. While those institutions which give graduate courses have been listed in Appendix
II, many more beside these offer undergraduate work in these fields
and the total number of posts is large, varying considerably, however, according to the field of specialization.

Museums: The number of posts in museums, while less than that
in the universities and colleges, is still considerable. Federal, State
and Municipal museums have already been mentioned; many universities also have museums, often used primarily for teaching
purposes, but sometimes having a sizeable staff. The number of
museums throughout the country is very large, and the trained
archaeologist, especially if he has additional training in History of
Art and in Museum Administration, can fill a directional or curatorial post in one of them.

Field Archaeology: Except for archaeologists specializing in the
American field, few members of the profession can hope for a

career devoted entirely, or even in large part, to Field Archaeology. Most of the Federal and State posts are for work largely in the field, and many museums which conduct excavations in the Americas afford wide opportunities for such work. However, the number of expeditions sent outside the Western Hemisphere by American universities and museums is comparatively small. They are usually of limited duration and have small staffs of Americans, affording only few and irregular opportunities for participation in field work. Yet many students training in archaeology will have some possibility of excavating in connection with the programmes of the American Schools, described in Appendix III; a few will have the chance of continuing this work as staff members of the Schools.

Salaries: The salaries of archaeologists, in whatever field they choose, and whether they be employed in universities, museums, or by federal or state governments, will be roughly the same and will be about equal to those of university instructors in general. While scales vary with the fluctuation in living costs, the present salary scale will begin with approximately $4000 and will reach $10,000 for top posts, with some positions commanding higher salaries.

Fellowships, Scholarships and Grants
      While there is only a small number of fellowships and scholarships reserved specifically for students of Archaeology, there are many which are available to them as well as to others. In the first category are included the fellowships to the American Schools abroad; those of each School are listed in Appendix III. Some universities and colleges also offer fellowships and scholarships for study at the American Schools, such as those given for Athens and Rome by Bryn Mawr College, Harvard University and the University of Chicago. Among the awards in archaeology and related fields are:

AMERICAN NUMISMATIC SOCIETY: Summer Seminar in Numismatics. Grants-in-aid of $500 each are offered to students in the United

States and Canada who will have completed at least one year's graduate study by June in Classics, Archaeology, History, Economics, Art or other humanistic fields. Applications must be filed by March 1. Further information may be obtained from the office of the Society, Broadway between 155th and 156th Streets, New York 32, New York. Fellowships offered to university graduate students working on topics in which the use of numismatics plays a significant part. Students must have attended one of the Society's Summer Seminars. Stipend $2500. Candidates will be named by Deans of university graduate schools; no individual applications accepted.

BOLLINGEN FOUNDATION, INC.: Fellowships for research, usually in the fields of anthropology, archaeology, mythology, sociology, psychology, religion and art. Stipends range from $1200 to $3600 a year. For information address the Secretary, Bollingen Foundation, Inc., 140 East 62nd Street, New York 21, N.Y.

METROPOLITAN MUSEUM OF ART: Fellowships for intensive study in one or more departments of the Museum, plus a minimum of two months study abroad. Open to men and women who have completed two years of graduate work by June in the history of art, archaeology, or museum training at a recognized American college or university. Fellowship stipends are $4000 for a period of one year beginning July 1. Closing date, February 15. Address correspondence to the Dean of Education and Extension, Metropolitan Museum of Art, Fifth Avenue at 82nd Street, New York, N.Y.

WENNER-GREN FOUNDATION FOR ANTHROPOLOGICAL RESEARCH: Fellowships, grants-in-aid, etc., awarded to institutions and individuals for research and education in the field of anthropology and related sciences. For information write to the Wenner-Gren Foundation for Anthropological Research, 14 East 71st Street, New York 21, N.Y.

Archaeologists are eligible also for some of the many fellowships given annually by a number of organizations. Perhaps the largest single programme at present is that of the

U.S. GOVERNMENT FULBRIGHT AWARDS FOR GRADUATE STUDENTS: Approximately 950 grants are available for graduate students in a number of countries, in many of which archaeological studies can be profitably pursued. For the pre-doctoral awards application may be made through the Fulbright adviser at the applicant's institution or through the U.S. Student Program, Institute of International Education, 1 East 67th Street, New York 21, N.Y. Fulbright post-doctoral grants for teaching or research in various countries are awarded through the Conference Board of Associated Research Councils, 2101 Constitution Avenue, Washington 25, D.C.

Other programmes of importance are offered by the following:

AMERICAN ASSOCIATION OF UNIVERSITY WOMEN: Graduate Fellowships for the completion of the dissertation or for continued research after the Ph.D. has been received. Fellowships with stipends of $2000-$4000 are open to American women. Closing date, December 15. For information write the Secretary of the Committee on Fellowship Awards, 1634 Eye Street, N.W., Washington 6, D.C.

AMERICAN COUNCIL OF LEARNED SOCIETIES: Fellowships to provide opportunities for younger scholars to pursue research projects in the humanities. The doctorate or its equivalent is required, and awards have an age limit of 45. The amount of the award will vary, but will not exceed $7000. Closing date, 30 October. Also grants-in-aid to provide funds for significant humanistic research. Stipend not to exceed $2000. Closing dates, 15 October and 15 February. Address correspondence to the American Council of Learned Societies, 345 East 46th Street, New York 17, N.Y.

AMERICAN PHILOSOPHICAL SOCIETY: Grants for post-doctoral research offered for the promotion of research in the fields of scholarship. In general these grants are not made for projects requiring long continued support. Awards are made by the Committee on Research at its meetings in October, December, February, April and June. Applications should be submitted at least one month before the date of the meeting at which they are to be considered and on forms obtainable from the Society. Address correspondence to the American Philosophical Society, 104 South Fifth Street, Philadelphia 6, Pa.

JOHN SIMON GUGGENHEIM MEMORIAL FOUNDATION: Fellowships for research in any field of knowledge or artistic creation in any of the fine arts. Awards are normally limited to persons of between 30 and 40 years of age. In general stipends amount to $5000 for twelve months. Closing date, October 15. For information write the Secretary General, John Simon Guggenheim Memorial Foundation, 551 Fifth Avenue, New York 17, N.Y.

UNITED CHAPTERS OF PHI BETA KAPPA: Mary Isabel Sibley Fellowship awarded alternately in Greek (language, literature, history, or archaeology) and French (language or literature). Applicants must be unmarried women under 35 years of age with demonstrated ability to undertake original research. The Ph.D. degree is not essential, but the candidate must have completed both residence and course requirements. The stipend of $2000 is granted biennially. For information address the Secretary, United Chapters of Phi Beta Kappa, 1811 Que Street, N.W., Washington 9, D.C.

In addition to fellowship programmes established on a more or less permanent basis, other fellowships are offered from time to time for study in various foreign countries. The student contemplating such study would do well to apply to the Institute of International Education, 1 East 67th Street, New York 21, N.Y. for information concerning the scholarships and fellowships currently available.

WOODROW WILSON NATIONAL FELLOWSHIP FOUNDATION: Fellowships for first-year graduate study, open to both men and women in United States and Canada. Candidates may not apply, but must be recommended by their professors. For information address the Woodrow Wilson National Fellowship Foundation, Box 642, Princeton, New Jersey.

APPENDIX V

Archaeological Societies

ARCHAEOLOGICAL societies may be divided conveniently into national and local societies. The majority admit all who are interested, but while national societies are concerned with particular aspects all over the British Isles and elsewhere, local societies are concerned with all aspects within their particular area.

NATIONAL SOCIETIES IN GREAT BRITAIN AND NORTHERN IRELAND

The premier national society of Great Britain is the *Society of Antiquaries of London*. Membership of the Society of Antiquaries is restricted to those who have already made a contribution to archaeological work. Election is by ballot, for which candidates have to be proposed by Fellows; no one can apply for admission. The Society publishes *Archaeologia* and *The Antiquaries Journal*, both dealing with all aspects of archaeological studies, which may be purchased by non-members at £3. 13. 6 and £2 respectively.

The following societies accept candidates duly supported by existing members. Subscribers receive the journals gratis, and in cases in which monographs are issued, usually are entitled to buy them at a reduced rate.

The Royal Archaeological Institute of Great Britain and Northern Ireland, c/o London Museum, Kensington Palace, London W.8. Subscription £1. 1. 0. Interests cover the whole country and all periods. Publication, the *Archaeological Journal*. Meetings held monthly in London. A Summer Meeting of one week is held at centres all over the country, and occasionally abroad, during which antiquities in the neighbourhood are visited. Members are permitted to use the library of the Society of Antiquaries.

The British Archaeological Association, 11 Chandos Street, London W.1. Subscription £1. 5. 0. Interests cover the whole country and all periods, with emphasis particularly on Mediaeval archaeology. Publication, the *Journal of the British Archaeological Association*. Meetings held monthly in London. A Summer Meeting of one week is held every year in a different centre, with daily excursions to places of interest. The Association has a library at 11 Chandos Street.

The Prehistoric Society, Secretary, Miss J. M. Bull, 16 Pembridge Gardens, London, W.2. Subscription, £2. 2. 0. Interests cover the whole prehistoric period, principally of this country, but the prehistory of other countries is also included. Publication, the *Proceedings of the Prehistoric Society*. Meetings held approximately monthly in London. A long week-end Summer Meeting is held in different centres, at which papers are read and sites visited, and a week-end Spring Meeting is held in London. The Society does not possess a library.

The Society of Antiquaries of Scotland, National Museum of Antiquities of Scotland, Queen Street, Edinburgh. Subscription £2. 2. 0. Interests cover the whole of Scotland and all periods. Publication, the *Proceedings of the Society of Antiquaries of Scotland*. Meetings held monthly during the winter. The Society has a library.

The Cambrian Archaeological Association, Gen. Secretary: Donald Moore, Esq., B.A., National Museum of Wales, Cardiff. Subscription £2. 2. 0. Interests cover the whole of Wales and Monmouthshire and all periods. Publication, *Archaeologia Cambrensis*. A Summer Meeting is held in a different centre in Wales every year, lasting about a week.

The Society for the Promotion of Roman Studies, 31–34 Gordon Square, London W.C.1. Subscription £2. 0. 0, student associates (undergraduates and postgraduates with tutor's recommendation) £1. 0. 0. Interests cover Roman classical and archaeological studies, including Romano-British. Publication, the *Journal of Roman Studies*, which includes annual summaries of current Romano-British archaeology. Meetings held in London and a number of other centres throughout the country. The Society has a joint library and slide collection with the Hellenic Society at 31–34

Gordon Square, which covers classical texts and commentaries and classical archaeology of all countries.

The Hellenic Society, 31–34 Gordon Square, London W.C.1. Subscription £3. 0. 0, student associates (undergraduates and postgraduates with tutor's recommendation) £1. 1. 0. Interests cover Aegean archaeology and Greek studies. Publication, the *Journal of Hellenic Studies*. Meetings held in London and other centres throughout the country. The Society has a joint library and slide collection with the Society for the Promotion of Roman Studies (see above).

The Palestine Exploration Fund, 2 Hinde Street, Manchester Square, London W.1. Subscription £1. 10. 0. Interests cover Palestinian, Biblical and allied archaeological and textual studies. Publication (in conjunction with the British School of Archaeology in Jerusalem), the *Palestine Exploration Quarterly*, and monographs. Meetings held approximately monthly in London. The Fund has a library and slide collection at 2 Hinde Street. Film-strips on Biblical history are available.

The Egypt Exploration Society, 2 Hinde Street, Manchester Square, London W.1. Subscription £3. 0. 0. Interests cover Egyptian archaeology of all periods and textual studies. Publication, the *Journal of Egyptian Archaeology*, and monographs. Meetings held at irregular intervals. The Society has a library and lantern slides at 2 Hinde Street.

The British School of Archaeology in Iraq, Secretary, 15 New Square, Lincoln's Inn, London W.C.2. The School, besides carrying out the functions of a school of archaeology, described in Appendix III, acts as the society for those interested in Mesopotamian archaeology in this country. Interests cover Mesopotamian archaeology of all periods and textual studies. Subscription £2. 5. 0. Publication, *Iraq*. An Annual General Meeting is held in London: the principal activities are in Baghdad. The School does not possess a library in this country.

The British Institute of Archaeology at Ankara, 16 Bryanston Street, London W.1. Minimum subscription £1. 10. 0. The Institute, besides carrying out the functions of a school described in Appendix III, acts as the society for those in this country interested in the archaeology of Turkey. Interests cover the archaeology and textual studies of the whole area included in modern Turkey, of all periods. Publication, *Anatolian Studies*, issued gratis to subscribers of £1. 10. 0. The Institute does not possess a library in this country.

The Institute of Archaeology of the University of London, 31–34 Gordon Square, London, W.C.1, has a small list of members, subscription to which may be permitted to persons outside the University. Subscribing members receive notices of all lectures and exhibitions at the Institute and an *Annual Bulletin*. They have access to the Institute's library and, so far as the teaching and research activities of the Institute's scientific and technical departments permit, work may be carried out for members. Members are entitled to certain reductions in the cost of such work and in the cost of the Institute's series of *Occasional Papers*.

LOCAL SOCIETIES

There is an archaeological society, in some cases combined with a historical or natural history society, in nearly every county throughout the country. There are also a number of societies covering smaller areas. Membership is as a rule open to all interested persons duly proposed by existing members. The scope of the societies usually covers all aspects of the history and archaeology of their area, with a bias varying with local interests; a majority deal especially with Mediaeval subjects. Almost all issue journals. Many have libraries, and some are responsible or partly responsible for the local museums. Some are active in carrying out excavations and other fieldwork.

It is not practicable to give a complete list of local societies and their addresses, as in many cases the society as such has no permanent address, and correspondence has to be directed to the secretaries, who inevitably change from time to time. Anyone who wishes to get in touch with a particular local society, or to know what society deals with a particular area, should write to the Council for British Archaeology (see below), for details.

In addition to the local societies, the extra-mural departments of some universities run archaeological training and research groups. Enquiries should be made of the nearest university.

THE COUNCIL FOR BRITISH ARCHAEOLOGY

Address, 10 Bolton Gardens, London S.W.5.

The Council is the representative body for all organisations, societies, universities, museums, concerned with archaeology in Great Britain and Northern Ireland. In addition to the central body, there are Regional Groups, which are combinations of adjacent counties, of which the activities vary in accordance with local needs. Membership of the Council is corporate and not individual, but a number of the services of the Council, listed below, are available to individuals.

Calendar of Excavations. A register is maintained of those wishing to take part in excavations, for which the fee is 3*s.* per annum. Excavators willing to take volunteers are asked to supply particulars. A list of these excavations is then circulated each month from March until September to those on the register. The Calendar also gives details of Summer Schools and training courses in archaeology.

Current and Forthcoming Offprints. The Council publishes in April and October a list of articles appearing in periodicals, which, if ordered in advance of publication, can be bought. The annual subscription is 5*s.* Subscribers are thus enabled to order copies of articles dealing with a subject in which they are interested, which are about to appear in journals they might not otherwise see.

Bibliography. The Council publishes an annual *Archaeological Bibliography for Great Britain and Ireland.* This gives a complete index and bibliography of archaeological publications and articles in journals during the period covered. The bibliography is arranged both by area and by period (the price varies).

Book-List. The Council has published a *Book-List* which aims at helping teachers to make use of archaeological material in teaching local history. The 2nd, revised, edition will be published during 1960.

Air Photographs. Copies of prints of the Air Ministry 1 : 10,000 aerial survey of Great Britain may be bought at reduced rates through the Council by members of archaeological societies. The present price is 3s. 6d. for prints 9 ins. by 7 ins.

American Archaeological Societies

There are several archaeological societies of national scope, and a great many more which are devoted to local interests. Membership is generally open to all who are interested, and for the student there is much to be gained by membership in one of these societies, as it will keep him in contact with recent discoveries and new developments in his field of interest. The principal national societies are:

Archaeological Institute of America. Sponsors the American Schools (see Appendix III). Publishes the *American Journal of Archaeology*, a quarterly for the professional archaeologist, and *Archaeology*, a popular quarterly intended for the layman. Offers lectures in all fields of archaeology through its nearly forty local societies. Holds an annual convention at which scholars present papers. Membership: Annual Member, receiving either *American Journal of Archaeology* or *Archaeology*, $15.00; Sustaining Member, receiving both these periodicals, $20.00; Student Member, receiving one of these periodicals, $7.50. The publications can also be obtained by subscription: *American Journal of Archaeology* $10.00; *Archaeology* $5.00.

For membership or subscription address the General Secretary, Archaeological Institute of America, 5 Washington Square North, New York 3, N.Y.

Society for American Archaeology. Publishes *American Antiquity,* a quarterly. Membership ($8.00) includes subscription to this periodical. Requests for membership should be addressed to the Secretary, David A. Baerreis, Dept. of Anthropology, Sterling Hall, University of Wisconsin, Madison, Wisconsin.

American Anthropological Association. Publishes the *American Anthropologist,* a quarterly, and *Memoirs.* Membership ($8.50) includes subscription to these publications. Address the Executive Secretary, Betty J. Meggers, 1530 P Street, N.W. Washington 5, D.C.

American Oriental Society. Publishes the *Journal of the American Oriental Society,* a quarterly. Membership ($7.00) includes subscription to this periodical. The Society has two branches, Middle West and Western, in addition to the main office in the east. For information address the Secretary-Treasurer, Ferris J. Stephens, 329 Sterling Memorial Library, New Haven, Conn.

Most of the states have state archaeological societies with which the student might profitably affiliate himself, if he is interested in American Archaeology.

INDEX

Figures in square brackets refer to plates